# STEPMOTHER

# STEPMOTHER

## A MEMOIR

by

MARIANNE LILE

SHE WRITES PRESS

Published 2016
Printed in the United States of America
ISBN: 978-1-63152-089-1 (pbk)
ISBN: 978-1-63152-090-7 (e-bk)

Library of Congress Control Number: 2016938633

*Book design by Stacey Aaronson*

For information, address:
She Writes Press
1563 Solano Ave #546
Berkeley, CA 94707

She Writes Press is a division of SparkPoint Studio, LLC.

Names and identifying characteristics have been changed to protect the privacy of certain individuals.

*For Art, my mom, and all three of my kids*

# AUTHOR'S NOTE

The word *memoir* always makes me feel I should be lounging on white satin sheets in sexy lingerie, casually eating chocolate and sipping champagne with my small white dog lying adoringly at my feet. This is not that kind of memoir. These are my memories of a slice of my experience as a stepmom. I have changed the names of most of the individuals in this story and on occasion have condensed certain incidents. Regardless of these changes, and with my lingerie folded away, I have built this as a true story based on my recollections.

# CONTENTS

# Prologue

## A FAMILY PORTRAIT

*O*NCE UPON A TIME, A long time ago, a handsome man asked a lovely lady to be his wife. They were married on a fair fall evening beneath the stars and the heavens. The joy of their friends and families surrounded them with love and blessings for health and good fortune. The sun set wildly, sending shoots of orange and purple into the sky. They were in love. They were fated to be together. With intertwined arms, they embraced each other and the circle around them. They glided out into the night, soaring toward the horizon and beyond, into the future, to live happily ever after.

Whoops! Stop! Freeze frame! I forgot to mention one thing: the lovely lady was now a stepmother. They floated out toward the horizon, into the bowl of ingredients society knows as a "blended family." A boy, a girl, their father, and me.

This is part of my story.

I

⚘

# FIRST COMES LOVE . . .

*T*HE HONEYMOON WAS OVER. LITERALLY.

We carried the last suitcase up the cedar porch stairs to the front door and dropped it on the family-room floor, and then—whoosh—with a kiss, my new husband left. Taking two stairs at a time, he hustled to his waiting car to drive to the Mother's house and pick up his two children. The twelve-year-old girl, Katherine, and the fifteen-year-old boy, Ashton—my new stepkids—would be here in forty minutes.

It was the fall of 1991, and this early November night would mark our first evening as a family in this house on the hill. My new home. I had the best of intentions. Don't most of life's stories start that way?

I was blinded by love—a love I had never before held in my hand. The kind of love you commit to and walk confidently alongside. *This love is different. This love is so strong. This love will result in magical events. This love will conquer the storms of life. This love will last.*

This love had begun almost two years earlier.

He had opened the door and shaken our hands, welcoming us to his office on the fourth floor of the state legislative office building.

"Hi. How are you?" my colleague said. "This is Marianne Lile, the new representative for the nurses' association."

"It's nice to meet you," I said, following her lead. "Thanks for taking the time to meet with us today."

He smiled. Taking my coat, this state representative from what was then the thirty-ninth district of Snohomish County pulled back the door and hung my coat up on the hook.

"Call me Art," he responded warmly. His green eyes were alert with an energy that said, *I'm listening.*

"How are you both today?" He looked to my colleague and me.

I guessed he was about six-foot-two as he pulled out chairs for us and then took his own seat, moving his office chair from behind his desk so he could sit in front of us. He obviously felt comfortable in his own skin, at ease with his height and strength. He had the look of an athlete, the kind of athlete who knows he has talent but doesn't brag about it, the one who wants the whole team to feel good.

We had been making the rounds of numerous legislative offices at the state capitol in Olympia, but this is the meeting I remember from that misty January day, though not for any obvious reason. It was a thirty-minute meet-and-greet to discuss our clients' legislative proposals for the upcoming session; we had done ten just like them. But this room was warmer. There was a spike in the air. The three of us spoke for half an hour, and then my colleague and I rose to leave. As he handed me my coat at the door, I felt it: The inexplicable. The undefinable. The mystery of connection.

"Thanks for coming by," he said as we walked through the doorway and down the hall.

He called me on the phone two days later.

"Hi," he said. "This is Art."

That same connection I had felt in his office, I heard in his voice. What is it about an initial bond? The buzz. The tingle. The inkling that it's there, and the huge gulf of not knowing why. The curiosity of it all.

I knew, even before he asked, that he was not calling me to ruminate on our legislative interests.

Running to the end of the common pleasantries, he said, "I was wondering if you would like to grab a drink with me."

"No," I replied instantly. "But thanks."

I had just started this job as a state lobbyist, and I was taking it seriously. I wanted to do well. I believed in my issues and the nurses' association that employed me. I had much to learn as a new face walking the halls of the capitol, and it was not on my agenda to have a non-job-related drink with a state legislator—connection or no connection.

The Washington state capitol is a relatively small place in a quiet town, Olympia, but once the gavel drops and commences the legislative session, the drama there unfolds with accelerated urgency. Every representative, every staff member, and every lobbyist moves around with supposed purpose, on their feet, walking and talking, sometimes bored, sometimes exasperated, sometimes beyond energized by some success. My first session in my new job in 1990 was a short one, sixty days, and it was thrilling.

The atmosphere around the legislative session is a bit of a bubble, mentally and physically. Everyone is in the same race, with similar timelines to meet. You see the same people in your areas of interest often, as you all attend the same hearings and meetings. You all speak the same language, hear the same gossip, breathe the same air.

After that first meeting in his office before the session commenced, Art and I saw each other frequently, albeit from a distance, around the capitol campus. He sat as a member on several of the legislative committees I was monitoring, and I often observed him walking through the "gulch," an area where the lobbyists stand idly around outside the doors to the capitol floor, waiting to talk to legislators. Tall and fit, sleeves rolled up once on his clean white shirt, he strode through the marble hallway, pausing to talk to other lobbyists. But it was mostly his eyes that I noticed. They delivered intelligence, interest, a gleam of humor. He was always polite, catching my eye. He was not flirtatious. He was merely persistent. And he kept phoning.

Perhaps it was the bubble atmosphere or the fast tempo of the workdays, but the initial link that had started only weeks earlier intensified. He had a particular energy to him that, coupled with his attractive perseverance, caused him to linger in my head.

One day, I pushed aside my hesitation and took a leap. "Okay," I said. "I'm free tonight. Let's meet at six."

I hung up the phone and immediately wondered why I

had agreed to see him; I had that push-pull feeling of being both excited and a tad irritated with myself for having let my resolve soften. But I told myself, *Okay. One drink. No big deal.* After I finished my work and headed to my car, I further reasoned that this "meeting" would end the curiosity and be the completion of this flirtation. *I'll just nip this in the bud*, I told myself.

WE BEGAN OUR CONVERSATION OVER a glass of wine at Budd Bay restaurant, a frequent destination for those of us working in the capitol; it was situated near the campus, on the pier next to the bay.

I parked my car and walked in. I was there first. I grabbed a booth by the front windows, ordered a glass of red wine, and looked out the window into the dark January night. The restaurant was not very crowded, so it was easy to see Art's blue Honda pull into the lot. I watched him as he walked confidently through the glass doors.

He sat across from me and smiled widely. "I'm glad this finally worked out," he said. He ordered the same glass of merlot I had and plunged right in: "What are you reading in your spare time?"

I noted, with a mixture of surprise and predictability, that we were both reading *The Mists of Avalon.*

From that very first question, our words came easily and fast. We talked philosophy. We talked more books. We talked world events. We talked and talked and talked. It was effortless.

Two hours later, two glasses of red wine ordered and

finished, we rose to leave. There was no kiss, we didn't even shake hands, but there was "something"—the connection that makes a smile appear as you drive home in the dark.

So much for nipping it in the bud.


THE NEXT THREE WEEKS WERE an adrenaline rush of phone calls and getting together. Our discussions were intense and consequential. Over seafood in Steilacoom, a small, historical town north of Olympia that sits grandly overlooking Puget Sound, we shared our visions of what we wanted for ourselves personally and what we were seeking in a long-term relationship. Art's fierce combination of high intellect and intense honesty drew me to him with a swiftness I'd never known.

"I'm looking for a single individual in my life," he told me. "I'm not interested in dating lots of women. Love is like food and drink to me. I believe without that connection—the physical affection, the bond—a person will starve. That's what I want," he continued, without apology or pretense. He had made hard decisions and sacrificed a lot for this ideal.

His description resonated with me. Food and drink—their essentialness; the sustenance they provide; being hungry for them, starved if you don't get them. It was a clear illustration of the human need for that connection, and his statement was filled with a vulnerability that was pretty darn sexy.

However, most recently, I had been in mostly blink-of-an-eye-short relationships, and my response reflected that experience: "I've seen only a glimpse of what you're describing, and it's never gone the distance. Part of what you're talking about seems to involve the intent of sharing it with the other person. I'm not sure I've met, or even been willing to share that level of love with, that kind of person yet."

I also told him about my previous jobs and my three years in Washington, DC, working in a lobbying firm on the Hill. I described my current life in Seattle and what had brought me back to the West Coast. I shared with him the story of my older brother, who had died a few years earlier at my parents' home, and the huge impact that event had had on my family and me. We each empathized with the deep emotional difficulties the other had experienced over the last couple of years.

We continued to meet every couple of nights, picking up the conversation where it had ended. Our commonalities were many: we were both idealistic, convinced that with the right person, the right love, the obstacles of life could be tackled. We loved politics and all its messiness and thunder, and both believed that good policy could be achieved in the system we worked within. We loved the outdoors and loved spending time both in the mountains and near the water. We loved food, all of it, from melt-in-your-mouth rare steaks to succulent halibut to bags of salty, finger-licking Cheetos. From the start, we were spontaneous, jumping into our cars, heading to some interesting destination we had heard about or a restaurant that had sparked our joint interest.

Art was confident without being boastful. He was generous. He was sure. I was someone who felt most comfortable putting up fences in my relationships. He barged right through those. He felt safe. He encouraged and pushed me toward my best self.

At the two-week mark, we met for sushi in Tacoma and I explained that I had never been a white-picket-fence kind of gal. I wasn't twenty-three and waiting to walk down the aisle of the neighborhood Episcopal church. I was quite receptive to a nontraditional sort of love and family. I was open to living in other places. I wanted to work and to achieve success. I imagined a family with lots of kids, mayhem, laughter, and love. And my brother's death when he was only twenty-nine had made me even more open to diving into happiness when it showed up. I knew firsthand that there were no guarantees in life.

"And now, here you are," I said to Art that evening.

"I WANT TO TAKE YOU to my family's cabin," I said to him on the phone one evening. "I'll pick you up in an hour."

We drove for four hours, listening to music, eating junk food to stay awake. The snow in the Methow Valley was so deep that year that his trusty Honda took several back-and-forth tries to get up the driveway to the front door. We lit a fire and poured wine and spent the weekend talking some more.

Our family log cabin, only nine years old, already had tons of stories to tell. I described to Art all the people in the pictures that lined the wall and their relationship to me. The old, scratched dining table that sat near the window had been my family's kitchen table when I was growing up. I'd played long card games, War, with my friends on the bearskin rug under the piano before we'd hung it there, over the log beam.

We trudged out in the knee-deep snow to the bench facing west toward the Sawtooth mountain range, where we had buried my brother's ashes. We looked at all the stars. It was our third week together.

"I love you," he said.

I was surprised and taken aback. As good as this union felt, I was not ready to echo his sentiment. He knew I wasn't ready, and he was okay with where we were.

My emotions were all over the place. I was deeply attracted to him, thought about him constantly, but I felt myself guarding against this intensity. I had known from the beginning that he was still married but had been separated for one year. His intention was to divorce, but he had not started the proceedings. I knew he was telling me the truth about the inevitable end of his marriage, but its lack of finality nagged at me, and I continued to date others, both because of Art's status and because I simply really wanted to. I was enjoying a new job, a different apartment, and a fresh outlook after some incredibly tough years. A door had opened, and I had walked through it, arms thrown wide, heart open.

My new job was a real opportunity for me. It was the kind of job you jump out of bed for. I had a knack for it. I liked the people I worked with, and I liked my boss; she was real, down-to-earth, someone I could respect. I loved the issues that I was allowed to advocate for on behalf of the nurses. It felt right. I felt like I was moving forward.

And I did date. A lot. Dating was fun. I accepted invitations for lunch, coffee, drinks, and dinner. I met all kinds of different people—young and old, smart and dumb—all of whom represented a common thread of much-needed enjoyment at that time in my life. I loved hearing their stories. We shared a lot of necessary and desirable laughter.

Despite my interest in and stubbornness about seeing other people, Art remained romantic and sensitive in the months to follow, even after the session ended and I moved back up to Seattle. He moved to his apartment outside Everett, thirty minutes north but still in his representative district. We took late-night walks in the snow and tried food of every flavor. We listened to live music and hit Sunday matinees. Blooms on Capitol Hill delivered flowers every single week to my office in Seattle with lovely notes about the preceding seven days.

Our age difference, seventeen years, bothered many. It brought up endless jokes and mumbles. I certainly considered it, but within minutes of being with him, I knew his age didn't bug me.

We kept our relationship very private. He was a legislator. I was a lobbyist. I was dating others. He had an estranged wife. He had two kids. All of these facts were reasons for our privacy, and we both felt strongly that the people on the near perimeter—his kids and his estranged wife—deserved this distinction until we knew what outcome, if any, this relationship portended. All this secretiveness did intensify our excitement, however. It was a little dangerous. A little decadent. A little untraditional. It was fun.

He knew what he wanted. To marry me. I was not convinced. For the next year, we stumbled over obstacles and questioned our motivations. He was patient, jealous, and generous. I was frustrating, funny, and hopeful. We questioned each other's values and mined our thoughts on our futures.

We talked about kids, the two that he had and loved very much and the several that I wanted. He began the process of legally divorcing. Slowly, the others I dated disappeared. We flew to Sayulita, Mexico, and took marathon walks on the beach.

"Yes," I said, "I will marry you."

And then, with the decision of a lifetime unveiled, it was time to meet his children.

Art and I had purposely waited for me to meet his kids until we knew our commitment was a long-term one. And even though we had decided to marry, we both knew that their approval was the last, and in many ways, most vital question in our relationship. These were kids he loved—they were not "baggage"—and they could make or break this promise he and I had made to each other.

"WHAT DO YOU THINK OF this outfit?" I turned to my girl-friend for advice.

"Are you kidding? Way too conservative," she replied, rolling her eyes. "Try this sweater instead."

The plan that Art and I had devised was for me to pick up all three of them at Mel's, the small diner across the street from the high school in their hometown, and head to my family's cabin for the long New Year's weekend.

As I drove to meet them, I rehearsed introductions in my head. *Hi! Hello. Well, howdy!* I guffawed at myself.

I stopped at an intersection, observing them through the windshield as I turned into the parking lot. They were standing on the curb by the door to the diner. Ashton and Kate looked nervous and self-conscious. Art waved to me as I drove in and parked.

I stuck with a simple "hi" as their dad made the introductions.

"This is Ashton. This is Katherine."

We shook hands.

"It's great to meet you. Your dad has told me a lot about you." I smiled.

I watched as they hesitantly climbed into the backseat of my car and we started the four-hour drive over the mountains.

I swallowed deeply and looked in the rearview mirror as we headed up Route 2, toward Steven's Pass.

"Your dad said you just saw *Total Recall*," I asked Ashton. "Did you like it?"

"Yes," said the blond-haired boy, with distant enthusiasm and a polite smile, quickly glancing toward me and then away again, not sure whether to look at me or gaze out the window.

"How's your basketball team doing? What position do you play?" I asked Kate, the quiet girl.

"It's okay," she mumbled, looking at me in the rearview mirror. "I play guard."

I studied their profiles as their dad continued the conversation, until sleep took over the backseat.

HOW COULD THE WEEKEND HAVE been anything but awkward? They had never seen their dad with anyone other than their mom. Art and I were by no means affectionate with each other, but I was clearly "the girlfriend."

"How are you doing?" he murmured while I washed a frying pan after dinner. Art could feel my nervousness, and I could feel his hopefulness. We glanced at his kids while they watched TV.

"Do you think they like me?" I whispered back at him.

"Of course." He smiled, looking at me in the reflection of the windows above the sink. "Don't worry. Just be yourself."

The fire crackled in the main room, and the television droned. We chatted mindlessly as we dried the dishes, slowly backing off into our own big thoughts.

I hadn't been around teenagers since . . . well, since I was a teenager. I had forgotten that they left plates to be cleared and wet towels on the floor. I remembered how body language could say a million things. I recalled the feeling of not wanting to be somewhere but being forced to attend.

I hoped they would be less nervous by the end of the weekend than they were when we started. I wanted them to like me just a little.

We pretended fun with card games and had a snowball fight on New Year's Eve. We stoked the fire and read our books. We stole looks at each other from across the cabin's rooms. We watched *The Shining*, made bacon, ate pancakes, and drove home with a big sigh.

"Hope to see you soon," I said, as they grabbed their bags and closed the car door.

"Uh-huh."


AFTER THAT FIRST MEETING, THE four of us saw each other fairly regularly. The next legislative session had started, and I commuted between Olympia and Seattle, meeting the three of them for movies or dinner on the weekends. At the end of the session, I had more time available, and with each meeting, we found more common ground. We ate pizza and went swimming in the river. I took them to my parents' house for sailing and barbecues. We laughed.

"All right," my dad said. "This should be a good spot to watch from." My mom came up from belowdecks with drinks for all of us. It was Seafair Weekend, the annual Seattle summer celebration capped off with hydroplane races on Lake Washington, a huge party with thousands of people eating, drinking, and meeting, and we had motored out on my parents' sailboat to join the hordes on the water to watch the Blue Angels perform their air show.

The action on the lake was pretty rough-and-tumble when I looked at Katherine sitting next to me. "Uh-oh."

She was going to throw up. My dad saw it, too. She was trying so hard to hide it.

"Hey," I whispered, "do you want some 7UP? It helps." She shook her head.

"Okay, then—you need to trust me on this—we're going to jump in the water. It will make you feel better."

She looked at me apprehensively. There were boats and people all around us. Katherine shook her head, growing paler with each passing moment.

"I promise," I said, grabbing her hand. "We'll go in together."

She stood slowly with me as I unlocked the latch on the gate to reach the edge of the boat.

"Are you ready?" I looked at her. "Now, we'll go on the

count of three: one, two … oh yeah," I said, looking at her and smiling, "try not to think about all the people using the lake to pee in." I jumped in, pulling her with me.

She bobbed up from under the surface. "That's gross," she said, but she was smiling. She felt better already.

WE MOVED SLOWLY, LEARNING NEW things about each other. There was no sense of urgency. Katherine liked her bacon really, really well done. Ashton liked to please. They clearly loved their dad and enjoyed being with him. They joked with him, made fun of his driving, pushed him in the water. I knew they had been hurt, but I didn't see a lot of tension or anger from them during that pre-wedding time. I saw shyness. I saw engagement. I saw glimmers that they liked me, even a willingness to make fun of me on occasion.

They seemed agreeable as we told them we would like to get married. They even seemed a little excited. The first nine months after that New Year's Day weekend were not hard. We did not have any big disagreements or major struggles. Art and I tried to keep it light. We planned fun things to do on each visit. It was an event. And after each event, I went home to Seattle.

Surrounding Art and me during those nine months were some big decisions and big issues, however. It became apparent fairly soon, during my second legislative session representing the nurses, that my impending marriage to Art was not going to meld easily with my job, not only because of potential professional conflicts of interest but also because of distance- and time-related logistics. Art and I planned to stay in the town, thirty-five minutes north of Seattle and an hour and a half from Olympia, that had been home to Katherine and Ashton. He and I both sensed a need, and I felt a strong desire, to be more present, especially in the initial months that would follow our marriage and the four of us living all together. If I stayed with this job, it would require a ton of driving and numerous evening events. It was not what Art and I envisioned for our life. Despite my real enthusiasm for the work, it felt better—felt like the right decision—to resign. So I did.

Art's formal divorce proceedings had started the previous year. He was not anticipating drawn-out negotiations, and I took him at his word, so we picked a date for our wedding and booked a golf club to host the ceremony at the end of October. My mom and I went shopping for a dress, and we both decided, with a smile and a good deal of laughter, that I was not a traditional, white-formal-gown kind of gal. The short black skirt and elegant white silk top I settled on were more my style.

The conversations between Art's lawyer and his wife's lawyer progressed. Art described positive conversations with her. All seemed to be moving along. And then they stalled. Art's wife had a good attorney. Some might have called him a ball-buster. He had an advantage based on the fact that Art and I had set a wedding date and started making plans. And despite the fact that there was very little that Art and his estranged wife did not agree upon, the proceedings dragged on and on and on.

"Any progress?" my mom asked me as we drove to meet the florist one day.

She was trying to keep it light, but my mom doesn't really do light. I knew my parents well enough to know they had concerns about the direction the divorce proceedings had taken. I tried to reassure them, but I felt the pressure, too.

I stressed. I didn't sleep. There is no good way to ask someone, "Are you divorced yet?" It was a worry, and it held a degree of sadness for all of us. Getting divorced is not fun—even if you are not the party doing it.

Art assured my parents and me that the process of ending his first marriage would be done in time. I chose to trust him and keep my head high. I was certain that Art was going to get a divorce even before he met me, and before we had picked a date to get married. It was going to happen with me or without me.

So we forged ahead. We made guest lists and chose the flowers, and eventually, after much negotiation, the final papers were signed at the end of the summer—about eight months longer than we had ever anticipated. I was sorry for Ashton and Katherine. I was sorry for Art. It was not ideal.

But I also knew that I had shown—demonstrated to the best of my ability and with no pretense—through all the months since New Year's, that I was all-in with Ashton and Katherine. I had looked forward to getting together with them. I really liked them and enjoyed their emerging personalities that they shared with me. I was as committed to them as I was to their dad. We were all going to be together as a family.

And so we were married.

NOW, HERE I WAS, HOME from our honeymoon, going to bed with their dad and staying for breakfast. My toothbrush was in the bathroom, and my hair dryer was on the shelf. I was there for good. I wasn't driving back to Seattle.

I grabbed the gifts that we had brought back from our trip and waited for them all to show up. I looked around at this shell of a house. These two had lived here with their mom and dad, but now it was empty of furniture and pictures. Walking through each room, I designed and imagined. My family. It now included a dog, three cats, a mortgage, and dirty socks. Most important, it included his two children.

Art and I had talked about step-parenting in the months prior. We had envisioned the dos and don'ts of this new relationship. We had had general conversations that felt like magazine article titles.

"Don't step into the role of disciplinarian."

"Give them space, time to adjust."

"Don't throw a million changes at them at once."

"Be patient."

"Show them that you care."

But on this day, this first day, the actual reality of becoming a stepmother was feeling a lot different than the conversation we had had about it.

For one thing, it became *it* the minute we signed the marriage certificate.

There is no ceremony for stepparents. No stepmom shower. No waiting for the official papers as you would for an adoption. No party balloons. All of a sudden, you are standing at the doorstep of life with people who have already had parents who lived together in the same house.

I mixed the salad and checked the potatoes in the oven. The steaks would be ready to cook when they arrived. I kept checking the clock and walking from room to room. Finally, I heard the car in the driveway and went to open the front door.

"Hi!" I cried.

It had been two weeks since the wedding, and I had a genuine hug of enthusiasm for each kid.

"How are you guys? Are you all hungry? Dinner will be ready in a little bit."

The conversation continued as they told us about school and soccer and we described our trip. The white beaches. The blue sea. The incredible snorkeling we had done, where we had seen multiple kinds of tropical fish and elaborate coral.

"You guys would love it," their dad told them. "I can't wait to take you there sometime!"

It was our first dinner together, married and blended.

We all pretended this was normal.

Later that evening, I gathered the three members of this new family on my old living room couch and the camera clicked. As we recorded our first night, all as one, everything seemed sort of, maybe, possible. And while I did not expect it to be easy—nor did I expect way back then that those two kids would feel the same way about me or our marriage as I did about them—I did imagine a time when it would simply work.

# 2

## OUR TOWN—NOT A STAGE PLAY

*T*HERE WAS NO WELCOME WAGON when I moved to our little town.

And I had not yet met the Mother.

In the fall of 1991, when I moved in and arrived at my new home after our wedding, she lived twenty minutes away, on the other side of the town, which was divided by an old main street and a highway that took you to the mountains or the city. Her new, white house was a short drive, winding past the Ben Franklin craft store and the Safeway, from the two schools her kids attended.

Without missing a beat in those first weeks of marriage, I had been elevated to primary chauffeur by my nonworking status, and I was now familiar with the Mother's cul-de-sac, her neighbors' houses, and her small, sloped driveway.

I started the car that late afternoon and headed down our steep drive. Hitting the flat, I wound around the turns on the rural road to town. The llamas all looked up as I drove past the farm on the corner and headed toward the pickup spot at the school gym. I was early, and as I sat parked in the lot, I looked with open curiosity at all the other cars pulling in to pick up their kids.

Ashton was first to open the gym door and head out. He lumbered over as Kate turned the corner with her friend, parted ways, and walked in our direction. I smiled at them as they came over to my blue Volkswagen, threw their sports bags in back, and got in. Hunger and fatigue followed them like flies and settled in the car the minute they closed the doors. All of us locked, belted, and trapped, I put the car in first gear and the boy, the girl, and I headed out of the lot.

The niceties were quick. Me: "How was your day?" Them: grunt, sigh, "fine." Then the fingers reached out to change the radio station, signaling the end of that conversation. My role as chauffeur was still new and not quite comfortable or normal for any of us yet.

The plan on that crisp, sunny November day had included my dropping off the kids at their mom's house after their sports practices. As I turned left and reduced my speed toward the end of the cul-de-sac in her housing development, we all saw a figure in the driveway. Dressed in slacks and a blouse. With a broom. Sweeping the leaves.

I took a deep breath, pulled in, and turned off the ignition. I knew this meeting was inevitable, but all I could think right then was how nice she looked for sweeping leaves.

I opened the door of the car, got out, and smiled. "Hi. I'm Marianne."

"I'm Vicki," she replied. "We finally meet."

My conversation with her was similar to the one I had just had in the car with her children: short.

As we finished our introductions, the kids opened the trunk and began grabbing their bags. My quick-footed stepson was in and out of the car in thirty seconds; my blond stepdaughter, taking more time than usual, was observing every single expression and movement. The meeting was over. The relationship began.

Let's face it, it's a weird relationship. I was now married to the man Vicki had married. I made her kids dinner. And, frankly, those were probably the only reasons we now had to have some sort of connection.

I know I wanted unconsciously for her to like me, accept me, think I was a good influence. In the weeks and months that followed, there were days when I even felt a tad like I was courting her, inviting her to the ball. Other days, a sense of dread came over me. I tried to put myself in her shoes and understand, but then it felt like pandering. I did not necessarily experience animosity from her, but I don't remember a lot of generosity, either.

It wasn't like we talked often, if at all, though. In those first months, the kids' schedules drove our interactions, and for the most part she and Art created the responsibility list for each house by phone.

In fact, it was this lack of conversation that set the tone for the relationship. There was none at weekend soccer games, when we stood yards away from each other. None during the week as I dropped off the kids before she got home from work. The silence was significant in what it did say. And it was a forced connection; I had chosen this relationship, but neither the kids nor their mother had chosen me—or anyone, for that matter.

When Art and I married, I moved into the house that he and his first wife had built and lived in for many, many years. They had made the decision he would take the house. Together, we had made the decision to live in the town where his kids attended school and that was central to all of their activities. I embraced these new decisions with excitement and optimism. They felt right.

When I moved there, it was a very small town, with fewer than five thousand residents. My husband was a pretty recognizable face. He was a local doc, and when we married, he was still a member of the state legislature. He had knocked on pretty much everyone's door—literally.

This house sat on the top of a rugged hill that rose 750 feet. Art loved the place—the hill, the land surrounding it, and the house. Years before, digging through Metsker Maps in Seattle, he had found the spot, approached the owners, and, over time, bought each parcel, which in the end totaled sixty-nine acres. He had bulldozed the driveway and helped dig the ditches for the underground electrical wires. He had dragged and shoveled every rock, every pile of dirt, and each individual fir-wood beam that had gone into creating the space. It was a love affair with a piece of property. He thought about it, nurtured it, and cajoled it. My love affair with Art meant throwing myself into this place, too.

The house sat on solid, volcanic rock, surrounded by grassy pasture, nettles, ferns, and forest and offering views of the surrounding valley, Mt. Rainier, and the Olympic Mountains. The central meadow had a pond with trout, and from the surrounding forest deer appeared silently, only to scatter when they heard car wheels spinning on the gravel road. Some mornings, eagles came out, disguised as Snoopy and the Red Baron, dogfighting with the wind and each other. The driveway up to the house was long—one mile from the bottom. It was also steep. My ears popped whenever I drove up it.

I loved it that fall, as the fog lay below the house and the sun drenched our windows with heat. The huge maples were dropping the last of their red and orange leaves, and the night sunsets, colors behind grayish-white clouds, whispered, *It is beautiful out here in the world. Anything is possible.*

The joint custody agreement between Art and the Mother was every other day. Yes, every other day, this boy and this girl were at a different house—ours or hers. And then every other weekend. This custody shuffle was tough. There was always something left at the other house: notebooks, saxophones, soccer shoes, a favorite pair of jeans—not to mention memories and a parent.

Of the three adults in this triangle, I was the only one not working. Vicki had recently started a new job, and Art had returned to his medical practice in Everett. The location of our houses, the kids' schedules, and the basic realities of life dictated a lot of driving. Carpooling was not convenient, and the conversations remained short and jagged, but as the weeks flew by, I began to sort of like it. From the window of the driver's seat, I could match the faces of friends that went with the names I had heard. I observed the jostling of teenage hierarchy as the kids opened the doors of the school building at the end of the day and headed to their various pickup spots. I got to overhear the gossip, and I began to recognize their

STEPMOTHER

rhythms. I learned all the new, hip songs and spoke with familiarity the names Jordan, Jonathan, and Donnie—otherwise known as members of New Kids on the Block.

I also began to identify old family friends. This driving schedule meant that most of them had seen me. I use the word *seen* on purpose—most of them would not talk to me and even went out of their way to avoid me. Walking down the aisle of the sole grocery store in town one afternoon, I actually saw a woman turn around and retreat after she entered the aisle, glanced up, and saw me coming toward her from the opposite end. I often felt as if I were the lead character in a horror movie, in a scene that depicted me walking down the street while the citizens of the town recoiled.

I had not anticipated how often I would see these old friends. I had not looked at the kids' incredible schedule of activities before I moved there and began figuring out how long it took to drive to all those playing fields and school parking lots.

I might have sensed that something was a little off—that the community was not really receptive—before we were married, but, for the most part, my interactions with Art in the months prior had been in Seattle, or Everett, where Art had an apartment, or somewhere in between. We had spent no time in group settings in his world.

And, don't forget, I was in love (sometimes also known as blind and dumb).

So when Art and I suggested to the kids before the wedding that if they wanted to, they could invite a friend, it did not occur to me that this might pose a problem. "You can ride in the limo, eat cake, dance ... It'll be fun!"

27

"Oh. Okay," said one. "I guess that would be okay," said the other.

Ashton invited a friend. Katherine asked her closest friend, then her next-closest friend, then her next one, and so on. They were all busy on that day. Finally, one said yes. Navigating a hundred other details, I did not pay much attention. I had seen this friend at school but had never really met her.

"Great!" I said. "I'm glad she can come. Do I need to call her mom and explain anything?" I asked Katherine.

"No, it's okay," she replied.

As the weeks after the wedding passed, I kept trying to encourage this same five-foot girl to have a friend over to the house, spend the night, do girl things. No one could ever make it. And then came the aha moment: these kids from town were not *allowed* to come over and mix with the new situation. The pages of the books of my childhood flew open in my mind. I was "that woman." Poisoned apples and everything.

I was thrown.

I had not put any thought into whether the community at large would like me or how they would treat me and our new family. It was not even on my radar. I had been the new person in towns before and had just figured it would take time to meet people. And Art and I were focused on us—the four of us. Most decisions started from that premise: What would be best for us?

The pieces started to fall into place. We would go to soccer games. I would stand with my new husband, alone, on the edge of the field, watching the action. I would cheer my support and frown at bad calls. We stood there by ourselves. On weekends when he couldn't go, I stood alone, watching and feeling Katherine's anxiety as she tried to figure out whom to say hello to, whom to wave to, where to look, when she eyed the sidelines. I am surprised now, when I think back, that the earth didn't feel the imbalance of weight and lift up the ground like a teeter-totter as all the "real" parents stood on the other end of the field.

I was beginning to feel as if I were in some sort of no-woman's-land in this small town.

Art is strong and smart, and he has one character trait that has served him well: public opinion doesn't bother him. He looks at all the information, weighs the options, and makes his decision. He has immense courage in his convictions. He does not glance back. Like snow on a metal roof, barbs and criticism slide right off him. Not feeling the blackberry brambles, he is first to forge a new trail. To the exhaustion of his kids and spouse, he cannot hike the trail most hiked—there is always a more interesting route and something new to see.

I am not immune. Blackberry vines kind of bug me.

So he put his arm around my shoulder and said, "Don't worry about it. How long could this last, anyway?"

"Right," I said. "Just shrug it off," I mumbled to myself. "Besides, what does it really matter?"

Love, in addition to making me blind and dumb, also gave me an extreme dose of confidence. I hung in there and smiled and drove. I threw myself into the house. I scrubbed and painted. I cooked. The right side of my brain kicked into high gear, and I evolved into a regular Martha Stewart. I designed and cut my own stencils and added purple, magenta, and blue to the walls. I sewed cream-colored floating curtains for the skylights in the kitchen. I had us all sit at the dinner table with a different meal each night and attempt conversation.

As the months flew by, the shiny newness of that first week became a distant memory. My toothbrush was still in the bathroom. Ashton, Katherine, and I were still in the car a lot. The conversations were getting a little funnier and even, some days, a little longer. I was getting used to making my tomato pasta without extra-hot Italian sausage, and I was learning how to play Sega. I liked it. Sometimes I found myself practicing it for a minute (okay, a little more than that) so I could attempt to beat Ashton when he got home.

The days were full and busy. Even aside from the hectic schedule of teenage activities, the every-other-day custody arrangement kept all of us—Dad, Mom, Kid One, Kid Two, and me, the stepmother—in each other's lives very closely and dealing with many issues. We had different rules at each house. We had financial obligations that continued to intersect. We had voodoo dolls (okay, just kidding). We started having days and nights filled with tension.

It was as if some sort of light switch had been flipped. I looked at Art, Ashton, and Katherine and wondered what had happened to them. The easygoing nature of the summer months had changed into something I had not seen before. The kids seemed sullen and upset. Art was different, too. The attention to detail he had placed on us and our relationship had disappeared. His focus had shifted to his practice, and some days I felt as if he had simply checked a box—remarried, done; now on to the next project.

Our life at home on the hill was far from smooth or simple. It is hard to admit even now, but as early as only a few months in, I began to anticipate how each day would be based on the amount of interaction we were all going to have: *Am I picking up the kids today? Is it our day for them to come here? Will I have to do my dance with their mother today?*

Ashton and Kate, despite the warm-up to our marriage, were having trouble adjusting to the in-your-face reality of it. The prelude had been composed of "fun" events, and then I had gone home afterward. The reality did not involve constant fun, and I went upstairs each night.

If they were at our house, the night usually included my stepdaughter breaking down in tears, screaming at her father, calling her mother, and being on the phone for the next several hours. It could be an algebra problem ("You're not explaining it right!") or a tone of voice ("Yeah, right, Dad!") or a backhanded, snarky comment ("You're so mean!") that set her off and caused something entirely mundane to become another huge episode.

My stepson was there but absent, slipping off to bed. Many nights, Katherine, worn out from tears, crept into our room in the middle of the night, slid in next to her dad for a hug of comfort and reassurance, and slept with us until the morning.

The next night often included long conversations between Art and Vicki on the phone, rehashing the night before, as they attempted to design a path toward making sure their children would be okay. And, having not lost my own voice, I would have to contribute my thoughts on the subject. It was a whirlpool.

The community was not showing signs of fatigue, either.

The shift in the landscape still seemed too much for people, the hostility still clearly marked. These folks were angry at my husband for his wrecked marriage, and they looked at me with a mixture of curiosity, irritation, and infuriation. I could almost see the gnashing of teeth.

I began to look for those moments of solitude—not for any kind of peace, but just to be alone, to sort my thoughts. If the weekend included the kids, I found myself on Wednesday gearing up for some unknown. What would happen this Saturday? Would there be any conversation? Or would there be another argument?

It wasn't like I was moving in with people who wanted to get to know me. I was not going to be asked about my thoughts on the environment or what kind of dogs I liked. Instead, the eyes of teenagers were observing me constantly. I knew if I had put the dishes in a different place than the spot they had been in before. I knew if I hadn't bought the right snacks. I knew I folded their socks differently than their mother did.

I began always to start dinner by chopping onions and garlic, taking out my pent-up emotion on the cutting board, wet eyes over onion vapors. One night, looking at my pile of chopped ingredients, wondering if I could add more red pepper flakes, I heard the phone ring. There was no caller ID in 1991, at least not at my house. I heard that familiar tone of voice from my husband as he answered, meaning that the Mother was on the phone.

He sat down at the table in the solarium as they talked. "Sure, that will be fine," he said, as he walked back into the kitchen.

I looked expectantly at him. My husband, my Art, with his green eyes and strong shoulders. A still-lovely sight.

"Vicki has to go away this weekend for something. She'll be gone till Monday night. It's okay if the kids are here, right?"

"But you're going away, too," I said.

"Don't you think this might be good for all of you?" he asked distractedly, as he shuffled through the mail.

"I don't know …," I said, with absolutely no enthusiasm for the idea. I tossed in more red pepper flakes. But, as I already had many times before, I silently acquiesced to what I thought was the right thing to do. This was now my family, our kids. I was as responsible as anyone. And I had been volunteered to watch the kids for four days. By myself. On a weekend when I had been looking forward to having no one around. I had been planning on having my own private oxygen, but all of a sudden, I had the kids. So even though I told myself it was the right thing to do, I was a little pissed. So were they. We all knew we were all a little pissed. They closely resembled animals caught in the headlights as they wondered why their parents had abandoned them with me, the stepmother.

Talk about long silences—we had the television on all weekend just to create a distraction. We watched movies and did a school report in a shoebox. They retreated to their rooms and talked to their friends on the phone. I drove them to soccer and told myself not to worry when they hustled from the car and that nice old friend of the Mother's looked the other way.

If there was progress in this relationship, it was hard to

see and hard to categorize—the emotions were so complex, layered over each other, sometimes hiding, sometimes pushed to the forefront without warning, like kids shoving one child to the front of the group to face the other side. The layers were piled on so quickly those first months that there was very little time to strip some of them off and let air in. Outside the house, I felt on edge, never knowing what to expect, and when I was at home, I often felt frozen and confined, unable to express myself.

Those first months were heavy, and not because of the fog or the drizzling rain. Our house was not a place of protection or comfort. Instead of leaving the problems of the world behind when I opened the front door, I knew I was about to see new problems. It was impossible to escape the intense emotions: the Mother's, the friends', the kids', my man's, or mine. There was no space. It was a constant flurry of band, school, soccer practice, laundry, grocery shopping, and vacuuming.

The communication between the four of us vacillated between extremes, from quick updates to polite chatter to full-blown yelling. Just when I thought I was okay and could do this, some new event would transpire. Ashton could hardly look at me, much less talk, and Katherine fluctuated between a sweet, funny thing and a full-on dragon, spitting fire and wrath. Art and I were further and further apart.

The picture we had talked about when we'd described our marriage was hidden in the mist. I felt alone and isolated. Was I being too sensitive? Was I expecting too much?

One late afternoon, as dusk settled, I was driving along the road I had already come to memorize to the Mother's house, when I saw flashing lights behind me. "Darn it!" I sputtered.

Watching the police officer undo his seat belt and get out of his car, I heard a sound from my passenger.

"Here comes my mom," Katherine said. Our instant reaction was to both duck down.

Quickly, the adult in me kicked in (*Shit, what am I doing?*) and I popped back up. Caught mid-scrunch as the officer knocked on my window and the Mother drove by, I saw her glance sideways at my car.

The ticket said I was speeding, but the incident emphasized my feelings of doing something wrong and being out of place. This puzzle was not supposed to include me. No matter how many times the piece was turned in those first months, I felt like I was never going to fit in.

# 3

## BLEND BUT DO NOT OVERMIX

"Whisk the egg, canola oil, honey, and vanilla ...
Whisk in yogurt ... Whisk in flour mixture, stirring just enough
to bring the ingredients together.
Do not overmix, or the cakes will be tough."
—GREG ATKINSON, *West Coast Cooking*

*THAT'S IT!* I SHOUTED TO MYSELF.

Blend, but do not overmix. Do not overmix, or it will be tough.

I read that instruction and—bang!—that was it. I practically hit myself in the head with my wooden spoon. This was the key to the map I had never been given. I knew north, south, east, and west, but I had never gotten that simple instruction: blend, but don't overmix.

The old lobbyist in me kicked in, and in a simple poll I took with myself, I decided this was it—the instructions the biological parents never gave, the kids' wishes, the community's desire: *The reality of your actually being here in the same room with all of us has hit with a loud, obvious thud, and getting rid of you isn't going to be easy, so it would be great if you just sort of morphed in and out of awareness.* I could sort of be there, but not really.

I could be the driver if no one else was available. I could clean up after everyone. I could do the laundry. I could cook. Once in a while, I could pick the TV show. But I couldn't discipline, I couldn't tell the mother to get a life, I couldn't tell the townspeople I thought they were all nuts.

The pain of it all—of my being there—was overwhelming at times. I was the constant reminder of the ending of one family, a reminder that the kids' other parent was in another house, and not with them.

I didn't know it then, but this stepmom started with a deficit because I did not know the real history of this boy and this girl, the ingredient list that had molded these kids into the folks they were at that point in life, at ages twelve and fifteen. The real stuff. The stuff you don't really talk about. Not when they first walked or talked, but the bits and pieces that molded them to this current space, the real matter that made them unique. As a consequence, I did not always know how to respond to a given situation. I didn't always get the inside family joke. I did not know the story of that scar on his nose. I didn't know about nettle soup or the view from the porch before the trees grew up.

I did not know their family history. The stories that Art had told me and the small anecdotes that I had heard from Ash and Katherine provided me with a picture, but it could not ever be the same as being in that history together. We had no shared family history yet, and it is this kind of shortfall in the blended family that makes it especially tough.

Shared history makes getting through the hard times easier. You can bring up the funny incident when Dad tipped over the canoe, or the sad time when he accidentally killed the goat. In the traditional model, you would all have been in that together. It's the stuffing of the stuff.

Not only did my new, married family history not yet exist, but at the time I did not even think deeply about or clearly understand the importance of the family history of these three people. The family history that began when I, the stepmother, first entered the front door was at times bittersweet, ragged, and full of holes. There were tears; there was anger and tension. Despite the fact that they had known me for a while, and even sometimes liked me, these two kids were in pain about this new, blended family. It was not the same, not what they were used to, not what they really wanted. It did not have the same comforting rhythms. They proceeded with caution and apprehension. Sometimes they were all-in, and sometimes they chose to check out.

"WHAT'S THAT? I ASKED ART, not able to stop the words from tumbling out when I glanced at my new husband and his daughter. I clearly knew what it was.

A Christmas tree.

As a "surprise," Art had gone out and bought our first tree. It was just like the trees he had bought with family number one.

To be utterly candid, I am a Christmas-tree snob of sorts. It's a noble fir or it's not Christmas. But the fact that it was not a noble fir was not the main issue. We had been married two months, a rough two months, and I was looking forward to this first Christmas with my "family." Not the tree from family number one. Not the memories of Christmas past. I wanted to remember getting that first tree together. Without knowing the name for it, I wanted to begin our family history. We went back to town and got a noble.

I put the tree in a new spot. We did not have many ornaments, so I coerced Ashton and Katherine into stringing cranberries and popcorn. I pulled out my memory bank of Christmas and put on the Ray Conniff Singers and Barbra Streisand. In my head, and unfortunately for those around me, I belted out "Let It Snow" and "The Little Drummer Boy." I carefully pulled out my grandmother's crèche from the big Frederick & Nelson box, taking the wrapping tissues off each piece, remembering where the donkey, the sheep, and the king stood next to the barn. Pulling my cookbooks from the shelf, I pored over the pages, trying to find a brand-new Christmas delicacy that we could eat through the holiday—a delightful treat that I would make each year to come. I imagined the future reminiscences that the smell would bring back for everyone. I made all the Swedish cookies that I had grown up with, too, dream cookies and chocolate crinkles. I went to Ballard, the Seattle Swedish community, with my mom and bought *smorkaka* and kringle for Christmas morning.

We went overboard with the lights. It was Friday night, and school had just let out for the two-week holiday vacation. We sat at dinner—clam linguine with red peppers and pine nuts—and as the conversation slid closer to some confrontation, I said to the kids, with merry enthusiasm, "Let's hang lights from that tree outside your bedroom window so we can see them from the highway!"

"Cool!" "Maybe we should get a star and put it on top!"

All that weekend, we ran to the hardware store for extension cords, lights, and replacement bulbs and decorated outside. Late Sunday afternoon, after it got dark, we turned everything on and drove down to the highway. After a quick U-turn, we started back across the bridge over the Snohomish River. At that one moment, we all gazed up the hill and saw, way off in the distance, a twinkling tree.

"Yes!" we exclaimed.

High fives all around.

But that darn holiday—and all the holidays to come—still loomed ahead.

"Do the kids seem quieter than usual?" I asked Art over coffee on Monday morning before he left for work.

"I haven't noticed anything," he replied with a kiss, gathering his things to leave for work. "Let's get a movie for tonight."

They woke later that morning to the smell of bacon and French toast.

"Do you guys want to go shopping for your dad today?" I asked them.

"Sure, I guess," they mumbled, half-awake, eating and watching television.

We headed south on I-405 to Bellevue Square. This mall was so commonplace to me, I still found myself surprised the kids had not been there very often. Compared with the town they were growing up in, Bellevue, my hometown, was a big city. My parents still lived there, in the house I had grown up in. When I was a kid, Farrell's was the ice-cream spot and Frederick & Nelson, Nordstrom Best, Shakey's pizza parlor, and the John Danz theater were the mainstays. My first real job, at sixteen, was at A Deli, a small sandwich shop next to the mall. I had seen the ash in the sky from the eruption of Mount St. Helens in 1980 while standing in the deli parking lot. Over the years, the mall had been remodeled; it was now fully enclosed, the biggest shopping center in the area.

The place was mobbed with holiday shoppers. The three of us walked through the aisles of the department store, looking at the ties and wallets. They laughed at soap on a rope and the latest Chia Pet as we meandered through the different stores and down the crowded hallways from one end of the mall to the other. We picked out presents for their dad, talked about getting in line for a Santa picture, and listened to the songs of the holiday playing from the mall speakers.

When we stopped for an Orange Julius, it finally occurred to me what their quiet mood, the looks that kept passing between them, were about.

I turned to Katherine and Ash and asked, "Have you gotten your mom something yet?"

"No," they replied.

"Well"—I paused and looked at them—"would you like me to help you find something for her?"

They glanced at each other sideways, trying to know what to say. They slurped the Orange Julius. After a frozen few moments, Katherine replied shyly, "Yeah, that would be great."

Usually their dad took them to buy her gifts, but he wasn't there to volunteer, nor did I think he was going to. So I did it—I bought her a very pretty sweater. They wrapped it up and signed the card and took it back to her house, where, I assumed, it lay under the tree.

On this first Christmas, Art and Vicki had decided to split the holiday: Christmas Eve with us, Christmas with her.

What that really meant was Christmas Eve with my family, and that year included not just my parents, siblings, and nieces but also a big group of extended relatives, people whom Ashton and Katherine didn't know or really care to know. I watched them on the couch in my parents' living room, sitting next to their dad.

*They are so uncomfortable*, I thought sadly. Katherine was wearing the dress she had worn in our wedding, and Ashton had on some random tie of Art's. By then I knew their fake smiles, and I saw them show up as my aunt or my cousin went over to talk with them.

But the worst was yet to come. After dinner, we left Bellevue and drove quietly home, to their mom's house. It was dark outside, and her lights were on inside as we all stepped out of the car. Vicki opened the door and watched our sad hugs goodbye as we wished the kids good night.

"We'll talk to you tomorrow," Art said. "I love you."

That is my first memory of our first Christmas as a family. I don't remember conversation or laughter. I remember fake smiles and sad faces. I remember feeling relieved that this Christmas, our first Christmas, was finally over.

# 4

## RESOLUTIONS

*N*EW YEAR'S PASSED. RESOLUTIONS WERE made. I woke up with renewed resolve.

"This will be a great year!" Art and I practically shouted at each other. (Can't you just feel that fist pump?)

Now that the holidays were finally over, the routine of driving and school and sports and homework started up again as if it had never stopped. Within days, a stack of parental permission slips, field trip forms, and sports information flooded the counter.

"We have snack duty this week," Art said, handing me the basketball schedule.

School basketball had started, and soccer was wrapping up, and there was a slip asking if anyone wanted to host the end-of-season party. I thought it over for about two seconds, and then I checked that box. I would force this hand. Instead of standing alone on the sidelines, I would invite everyone over.

"What do you usually eat at these parties?" I asked my stepdaughter.

I had been to only one of these events before, and the food had not been what I focused on as I stood invisible in the corner. Katherine was anxious that I serve Costco frozen lasagna—meat, not vegetarian—like all the other party heads did. I acquiesced, though my favorite frozen food is not lasagna but ice cream.

I set up the snack table. I set up the pop table. I set up the wine-and-beer table. The doorbell rang, and the girls' soccer team and their parents walked through the front door and stepped into the family room. I waved to Katherine. Vicki entered behind her with one of her friends. Many of these people had been here before, and I observed their faces as they checked out the new paint and furniture arrangements.

"Welcome, everyone!" Art greeted each one with exuberance. "Wasn't it a great season? Help yourself to anything!" His usual confidence shone through.

Blah, blah, blah … the conversation swirled around me. People had greeted me, but it was still awkward. And more than that—it was almost mazelike; I felt as if I were running into the same wall at every turn. The big rooms of this house shrank, just as they did at sporting events when the Father, the Mother, and I were all together with these other parents. And that happened frequently; depending on the sport, we could be at the same gym or athletic field two, three, even four times a week.

The man I married, this dedicated dad, wanted to be in

his kids' lives. We went to the games, we went to the concerts, and we went to the parades. He met the teachers with their mom. They were still speaking several times a week on the phone, sometimes daily, about the kids and all their issues.

Most folks just did not know how to respond and often seemed to leave their civility at the door. They also appeared to have taken a side—the Mother's. They circled around Vicki like a protective wagon train. When she arrived at the party, she glanced at me across the room. Her face expressed a frozen acknowledgment, a deep-freeze hello that was hard to miss.

Community friendships are composed of several circles of commitment. The closest circle in are the friends you call all the time, commiserate with, and invite to your birthday. In the next circle are the ones you know because your child is good friends with their child—there's not much else in common. And the last circle … well, it's the last circle.

These different circles of people moved around my house and slipped into small, congenial conversations, eating meat lasagna. I slipped into the solarium, the room I found myself retreating to frequently, a room I thought of as mine.

"Thanks for hosting the party," an attractive woman from the second circle said.

I looked up at this mom and said thanks. These acknowledgments were so sparse that I remember every single one.

I watched the kids intermingle, smiling at Katherine and her friends. I had wanted to host this party in an attempt to break some barriers. I had wondered how long this could last, but there had been no thaw yet. Like a bull in a pen, I wanted to shake these other parents and shout at them, *Don't you see? Isn't it obvious? I like these kids—a lot!* But it seemed pretty clear that day that my bullish attempts weren't going to throw down the fences. I was overmixing, and it was tough.

Ash and Katherine were self-conscious. I was the only stepparent in this room. And though it was certainly not my intention to make them self-conscious, there was no getting around that simple fact. I was the odd one out by sheer virtue of my presence.

But what they didn't understand yet, and what even surprised me, was how much I liked this new role. I liked finding and creating new meals to cook that I hoped would appeal to them. I liked watching them at their different activities, remembering my own enjoyment of soccer and scoring goals. I liked watching them come down in the morning and hearing them get ready for the day. I worked hard to keep our conversations level. I worked hard to get them to crack a smile or, even better, laugh at some dumb thing I said or did.

Later that evening, as the trophies were being handed out, I scanned that room of unfriendly feelings, looking at each adult.

*At what point,* I wondered, *will they see that I truly care about these kids and stop this nonsense of not seeing me, not talking to me? Would it be easier for all of them if I treated these kids like furniture or rejected them? Would that be better for anyone?*

SIX MONTHS OF THIS MARRIAGE slid by, and the flow of our household remained stormy. The two *t*'s, tears and tension, were still residents. Every day, we woke up, had coffee, cereal, or a muffin, left for school and work, and trudged along like the rest of the world—trying, hoping, and waiting for a volcanic shift in attitudes and feelings from the community and from Vicki. There was no sense of movement from these entities, but Mother Nature kept up her rhythm and pace.

Our house resided in the "convergence zone," an area north of Seattle where the weather is a little rougher, louder, and wetter. The end of the winter can be like pushing a very heavy bureau across the room: you're looking down the whole time, hoping the furniture doesn't scuff the floor, and then you hit the other side. As winter steps back and the grays turn lighter, daffodils appear from nowhere. And then—surprise—rainy skies part one morning to reveal the most beautiful sunshine-filled day. Seattleites pull out their dark glasses at the first ray.

On the hill, the leaves started to appear on the trees and small, flowering plants finagled their way up between volcanic rock, lichen, and moss. Glacier lilies and purple camas appeared like fairies outside the solarium windows. Spring had never been my favorite season, but even I had to admit this was pretty outstanding. And all the clichés about spring notwithstanding, it did give me a renewed sense of hope and resolve. If these determined little flowers could burst out of that volcanic rock, I could, too.


I WAS CHOOSING MY MOVEMENTS pretty carefully in what I now inwardly described as "the hood"—stepmother-hood.

Some days I did not care. I strutted out the front door and went for it, put my glorious self out there in front of this small, little town. I wore my old clothes that were funky, fun, and different, and I didn't care. Other days, well, I slunk my little self out into the street and counted the minutes until I could hide back on the hill. The in-between days were about just gliding by, doing what everyone advised me to do: "just let a little time go by." Go to the grocery store and, if it was our day to have the kids, pick them up and take them to whatever practice or activity was on for the day. Do not expect conversation. Do not be alarmed if they run from the car as quickly as possible. Do not worry about the blank stares from the crowd.

Then May arrived. The second Sunday. Mother's Day. That weekend is, appropriately, always Vicki's weekend. What I did not count on was the awkwardness of it all. In many respects, we were still stuck in the polite stage, so nothing was said out loud. But once again, I was like the big ol' elephant in the room: *What do we do with her?*

I arrived home on the Monday after Mother's Day and walked in the front door. The bags I carried from the grocery store were filled with my latest culinary ideas. I walked into the solarium, and there on the table was a lovely hanging basket, complete with a pink bow.

Art had gotten off work early and, trying to do the right thing, had taken the kids to buy a present for me, from them.

"Happy Mother's Day," they said, almost in unison. They were so very uncomfortable. The insincere politeness of it all was overwhelming. We weren't ready for gift giving. We certainly were not ready for Mother's Day gift giving.

I glanced quickly at Art. He smiled gamely. We had had a strongly worded conversation about this exact scenario. I had pleaded with him to let it go, not to force the kids to get me anything.

"They will get me something when and if they want to," I'd said to him the day before, Mother's Day afternoon.

"Well, I don't agree with you," he had replied. "It's appropriate that they do something."

"Please, just drop the idea this year. It's too much pressure right now. I don't want anything."

Round and round we had gone, never reaching a final agreement. Clearly, he had made up his own mind.

But stepmother and Mother's Day are at two opposite ends of the street. Card shops are still trying to figure out the right wording. The whole announcement of it ("Happy Mother's Day, Stepmother") pretty much sums it up: you're in the crowd but not in the circle.

The problem with the whole day is the theme of acknowledgment—a sign showing that somebody has been seen or heard by somebody else. That is tough for stepmothers. If stepkids acknowledge that the stepmom is there or—let's go the distance—acknowledge that they care about her, they have headed into no-man's-land. There are not a lot of markers in this territory to help steer them through. And when you add the guilt factor of whether acknowledging your stepmom means you might not be acknowledging your mom fully, it becomes a little hairy.

We were overwhelmed by politeness and a desire to make this family scene work somehow. So we hung that beautiful basket by the front door. We hugged our awkward thanks, and Art and I watched as Kate and Ash scattered pretty quickly.

I gave Art the look. The *I know you tried to do the right thing, but I wish you hadn't this time* look. A mix of exasperation, love, and *why don't you ever listen to me?*

THE DAYS CONTINUED TO LIGHTEN, and I watched this first spring season outside my new residence reveal itself more and more each day. I looked up from newly painted walls and buffed floors as my attention was invited outdoors. My new ideas and hopes for this home turned outward. It was time to garden and make my mark on the landscape outside.

"Wouldn't it be great if we could have a pond out here?" I said to Art. I put my garden gloves back on and stooped to pet the dog. I had pulled the weeds around the old trellis and planted the pink rose, Cécile Brünner, that my mom had outside her living room window. My dad always picked a bloom for a boutonniere on the rare occasion when a tuxedo was required.

"Let's do it!" he said. "I bet if we took out the dirt and moss around this area, it would work. The dirt goes pretty deep here, and we can see if the rocks below could hold the water. This will be great!"

By the end of the weekend, we had dug around that gray-black spotted rock and created a marvelous pond with a pump and a trickling waterfall. We added three spotted koi fish and floating green water plants.

In the next weeks, we carried bucketfuls of dirt from the pile in the driveway to begin our side garden, which we planted with lupine, peonies, and dahlias. We placed Japanese maples in the pots in the corner and a miniature pink dogwood in the pot on the front porch. Every plant was a down payment for a future in this house.

That weekend in June was glorious. Afternoon sunshine was pouring through the limbs of the fir trees, warming up the dirt we had hauled in that morning.

"I need to run to the hardware store. Do you need anything?" Art asked.

"I'll go with you if we can stop at the grocery, too. I was going to get some chicken and barbecue tonight."

I left my gardening trowel, bucket, and gloves by the front door, and we headed out. When we returned. I put away the groceries, then changed back into my dirty jeans and went to finish up my earlier project. Katherine was home by then. "Hey," I asked her, "did you move the trowel and stuff?"

She didn't look at me as she replied, "My mom used it."

"Your mom?"

"I wanted her to see the new bathroom and stuff."

Invited by her daughter, the Mother had come into this house—and into my bedroom, my new bathroom, my dining room, my kitchen—to look at the changes we had made and talk about the flowers, and then, on the way out, had dug up some plants she had planted and now wanted for her yard.

"Are. You. Fucking. Kidding. Me!" I screamed at my husband. "This is it. I'm fucking done. I have had enough. Who the hell does she think she is? How could you let this happen? What is wrong with you people? You are all so fucked."

A haze of fury surrounded me. It was as if I were in another realm and Art and Katherine were behind a wall of glass. I saw Art open his mouth, and I suppose words came out. I watched as he reached out to calm me down, but he could not get to me.

The last months had caught up with me. I had scared my stepdaughter. I think I had probably scared the whole hill. It was bedlam. My husband got mad. My stepdaughter sobbed. The dogs hid. The dominoes were falling. The swelling of rage was intense.

Seconds. Minutes. Hours. How much time went by? *Focus. Breathe. Step back in.* I saw the people around me. My stepdaughter crying. "Everybody hates you and Dad," she bawled.

On and on she went, about her mom and her mom's girlfriends. All the nasty things they had said and she had overheard. *Midlife crisis. Trophy wife. Loser. Jerk.* I could not be angry. I had to settle her down.

"It's all going to be okay," I told her slowly, in a monotone murmur.

The tornado of emotions still swirled in my body, and I felt kindred emotions as I sat beside her. I knew she was starting to like me. This was causing much confusion and creating anxious tendencies as she tried to sort her loyalties. We sat side by side on the white couch and looked out the window.

*What to do?* I wondered.

My monotone voice spoke again. "It's all going to be okay," I repeated to her, wondering to myself if it ever could be. "I promise."

That evening, as Art "handled the situation" with Vicki on the phone, I listened and simmered. Certain taboos in the stepfamily world—like don't confront the Mother—were gnawing at every independent grain in my body.

I swallowed and I suppressed.
It was just another fucking day.
Except for one thing: I was pregnant.

5

CIRCLING

*I*T WAS A GOOD THING I was pregnant.

It grounded me. Centered me. Helped me to move on to the next day and the third month.

Worn out and exhausted from early pregnancy, I sat on the edge of the bed, my stocking feet on the floor. I ate stacks of Premium saltines and sipped glasses of water. I could not help but look forward with great anticipation and cautious optimism.

We were having a baby. I smiled.

"So, we'll tell them tonight at dinner?" I looked at Art one morning.

I'm one of those people who wake up, sometimes even in the middle of the night, and start thinking with a certain degree of excitement about what to make for dinner. I was thinking steaks. Maybe some orzo. Fresh strawberries for shortcake.

"Sounds good. I should be home by six-thirty. See you

later." After a quick hug of assurance, he hustled out the door, with the dogs following him down the walk to the driveway.

I got up and looked outside our bedroom windows. I was still struck by this view. It was going to be a clear day, and Mount Rainier was front and center this morning. There was a small breeze, and the top of the trees waved one way and back again. I walked downstairs and through the dining room to the kitchen.

I wondered what my two stepkids would think about a baby. Happy? Sad? Excited? Noncommittal? Should we have told them before that we wanted to have kids?

I shrugged to myself. It didn't matter. It couldn't matter. Of the many lessons that I had learned so far in this short marriage, one kept coming back: there were going to be decisions or actions that were not going to make everyone or anyone happy. If I let each one knock me down, I was going to drown in despair pretty quickly. This love gave me confidence. I had to try hard and not waver. I could not let any lack of enthusiasm knock me down, or I would find myself on the floor too often.

So I was thoroughly and beautifully excited for this pregnancy, for this baby-to-be and for all the hopes and desires attaching themselves to that miracle.

The day sped by, and all three family members walked in around six-thirty. I was out on the deck, heating up the barbecue.

"Hey." Art looked at me. His tie was loosened, and he gave me a wicked grin. He knew I was nervous about the evening.

We had talked on the phone a million times that day, going over what we were going to say to them.

"It's pretty simple, Mar," Art had teased me. "This is what we say: 'we are going to have a baby.'"

We both knew innately that when and if the tough part of the conversation was going to appear, it would come after that sentence. I walked with him as he went to change his clothes upstairs.

"So, you start it, okay?" I said.

"Yeah. It's going to be fine." He glanced down at me. "Don't worry. They're going to be okay about this." He grinned again and gave me a quick hug.

I was overly worried about everything these days. The water, the cat litter box, the Comet I used to scrub the toilet—anything that might affect this baby. Dumb things got underneath my skin. "Generic prenatal vitamins!" I cried in alarm at him. "These aren't the same ones I had last month. These aren't the 'real' ones!" My moods and hormones raced in every direction.

We sat around the table and talked about our days. The steaks were medium rare, and the orzo was mixed with a little Gruyère. The grilled zucchini was delicious. Art started in.

"So, we have some good news," he said to the kids. "You're going to have a new brother or sister!"

"Wow."

The excitement, to say the least, was a bit muted.

They exchanged that sibling look over bushy eyebrows that can be described only as *I knew this was coming*. I wasn't sure if that was a good thing or a not-so-good thing.

"The baby is due in January," he continued. "What do you guys think?"

"Wow."

*Think. What* did *they think?* I wondered later, as I finished up the dishes. The conversation had been pretty contained, without a lot of expression. Were they worried about their place, their spot in their dad's heart? Did they think they would have to babysit? Worse, were they mad? Did they even know what a baby was? I figured they were mostly just thinking about how it would impact them as teenagers. Plus, it meant their dad was having sex—not something any kid wants to think about.

For once, I let it go quickly, down with the water in the sink, as I finished the dishes and dried my hands on the kitchen towel. This pregnancy was here, out in the open, and we would have to figure out the rest as it came along.

I LOVED BEING PREGNANT. I ate fruit. I drank V-8. I rubbed cream on my tummy and went shopping for new clothes. And, as they all do, this baby grew daily, stretching, pushing, and turning, its little arms and legs poking me through the day. It was magic in the finest sense of the word. I had a not-so-subtle secret. I had someone in my corner all day long.

Someone in my corner when my stepdaughter still cried every night she stayed with us. Someone in my corner when my stepson was so polite it hurt. Someone to whisper to that this was all going to work out, not to worry, everything would be okay.

I did believe everything would be okay—but right now, Art and I were stumbling. We had, not so long ago, walked in stride with each other, basking in a partnership that felt very solid. But now we had hit an intersection, and it seemed like we had each turned in a different direction. We disagreed over issues more than we agreed on them. We were so out of balance, we needed a strong gust of wind to blow away the harsh words and frequent discomfort that we both expressed.

"Do you have to go to his game this weekend?" I whined.

It was supposed to be "our" weekend. Art and I had not been alone in what seemed like weeks, and I did not want to see the kids. I did not want him to see the kids, either. My hormones were raging. My stomach was growing. I felt caught between a rock and a hard place. And two character traits I despise—anger and bitterness—were beginning to show up a little too often for my comfort.

Where we had once been able to talk and talk and talk, it seemed all we could now do was simmer and agitate each other.

"I should go," he said. "I want to go."

Art's emotional backing and his strong work ethic were being pulled in all directions. Trying to support the feelings of the three of us and not take sides only resulted in his leaving shreds of his help in numerous places. He was pulled toward his children and pulled toward me.

"You always side with her!" they heaved at him.

"You're letting them get away with it again," I threw out.

"You don't listen to us," they scowled.

"Do you ever hear what I'm actually saying?" I pointedly asked.

"I hate you," they mumbled.

*You know, sometimes I don't even recognize you*, I thought.

"I am on all your sides," he replied. He was exasperated, angry, and vulnerable.

His position at his clinic was being threatened by toxic internal allergens and by his position in the legislature. This elected post, the state legislature, is considered a part-time position in Washington State, and the constant tug-of-war between the two jobs—physician and legislator—and the imbalance at home was proving difficult to manage.

Still, Art loved all of his work. The patients he saw every day were funny, eccentric, challenging, and interesting. He got great satisfaction out of analyzing their health problems and helping them to feel better. In the state capitol, the issue of high-quality and affordable health care was at the forefront (yes, we talked about affordable health care in 1992, too), and he wanted to continue his presence in the mix of that debate and contribute to the outcome. But our home was synonymous with "severe winter weather warning" and also needed his attention. With very mixed feelings, he took one out of the mix and decided not to run for office again. It was a tough decision for him, the kind of decision that you know is the right one but doesn't leave you feeling great.

In the short amount of time that we had been married, it seemed as if every single day had produced some fallout. In one world, you think this guy's divorced and you have married him and started your own life, but every conversation is about the mother/first wife, or the kids, or the town, as if they are newfound long-lost relatives. We were like the ants that kept marching one by one—hurrah, hurrah—and we got up each day, stepping forward, stumbling, stopping, moving to the back, and starting over again.

"I CAN'T BELIEVE YOU'RE HAVING a baby," my amused girlfriend said one day on a random visit up to the house. I had been the friend in the group who everyone thought would marry last, have babies last. Instead, I was one of the first.

"And you have a *lap* dog!" she cried.

We both stared at the Pomeranian puppy lying on the solarium floor, the last one from my stepdaughter's dog, which now lived over at the other house—a litter of six no one saw coming.

I laughed. "I know. I can't believe it either. This puppy, this baby—this all has to work," I said to her. "Tell me it's going to work!" I pleaded with mock sincerity.

"C'mon, look at my mom, Mar—she travels with my dad's ex-wife!"

I didn't see that happening anytime soon. This ex-wife was bugging the crap out of me. Her shadow was always lingering—in conversation, on the phone, in her children's eyes. She was in the closets and the attic as I moved through each corner of this big house and discovered boxes or pictures that had been left to find.

She had been upset about the baby. And there had to be another phone call to talk about it all. Did her kids know what she thought? Why did I care? Why did I let it bug me? All I knew was my reality.

Games were being played. Vicki had visited my husband's brother in California, telling us all she was on a weekend date. Letters from her attorney kept showing up in the mail. Something as simple as our house refinancing had become complicated when we had discovered she needed to sign off on the documents. A lien on the property that had been added to the divorce settlement right at the end continued to haunt us. It felt like every time we made a turn to try to set things in balance, we hit some wall in front of us.

And my stepkids, Ashton and Katherine, were angry. Really angry. And they were teenagers. They whispered under their breath and talked back. I called my mom one day and apologized for anything I had ever said or done as a teenager. She laughed and said, "You were my last one; I don't remember anything!"

One evening, it became especially clear that Art and I were the kids' targets on which to take out all that anger.

"Hey, starting tonight, you guys are going to have a dish night," he said.

"We don't have to do the dishes at Mom's," Katherine interrupted. "We never had to do the dishes before ...," she added, looking past me.

"Well, that doesn't matter. You're going to start doing them now," he said. "One of you will clear, and one will wash."

"But I have too much math homework."

"My science test is tomorrow."

"I had practice. I wasn't even here for dinner."

"I can't believe you're going to make us do this!"

"Why don't you do them?"

"You're such a jerk, Dad!"

On and on it would go, starting out as something stupid and escalating into accusations and rage, then tears and phone calls to the other house, where no one did the dishes.

My pregnant imagination went nuts with theories and conspiracies. I began to wonder what conversations these two were overhearing or had overheard in the past. And I suspected that the lack of acknowledgment by their friends' parents was taking a toll. Did they notice the blank looks and the absent handshakes? Was this lack of support of the relationship of husband and wife, of stepmom and stepkids, of dad and kids hurting them, more than any of us could see? We interacted with these people weekly—and it was hard to thrive all alone out there. And there were four people involved who were trying to thrive. And now an obvious fifth person on the way.

"What do you want me to do?" I confronted Art one evening.

"I can't discipline the kids."

"I can't talk to Vicki."

"I have to listen to your kids scream at you, and I'm not supposed to say anything about that or how they don't do anything around here? I want to feel like this is my home, and I don't."

He didn't have any good answers. And those green eyes that usually so delighted me now rolled in frustration and exasperation.

"You're being ridiculous, Marianne. Please, just get over it."

Our humor had left town and wasn't even sending postcards. Our only conversations were about the kids, the finances, the Mother, and the town. From the moment we woke up until the moment we went to bed, the compass just kept spinning.

But each evening we did go to bed. And we always came together as if we were on a single mattress. Even with my growing stomach, we spooned every single night. We slept with love, and we woke up most days with hope and resolve to get through it. Past the sadness and the anger and the disappointment.


SUMMER.

Thank God for the end of school and the start of summer vacation. And, double thank God, my two stepkids liked sleeping in. I let them.

Those first days of summer presented the three of us— Kate, Ashton, and me—with a new routine. They were with me all day. They had to rely on me for transportation, food, and, yes, conversation. In many ways, it was a test for all of us. I found myself digging deep for creative inspiration to make the days go well, or at least smoothly.

And it was time to rally for another holiday: Father's Day. This one was easier. We could do it on our family's terms. I opened up *Gourmet* magazine to an article on a Vietnamese dinner.

"What do you think of this, you guys?" I pointed to the pictures, showing a feast of bright mango salad, shiny rice noodles with lemongrass, and a juicy grilled-beef concoction. A shrug of teenage shoulders was my reply.

"Have you guys ever been to Uwajimaya?"

Kate and Ash were watching television and eating breakfast. It was a typical late morning, without much response from my crowd. I knew well enough by then that conversation would be better after they ate. I gathered up the newspaper and waited.

Uwajimaya, a Japanese grocery store located in southeast Bellevue, was the key. It would be the outing for the day. I found myself always thinking about and searching for an excursion that would be different, an activity that would fill the silent gaps in conversation that we sometimes fell into.

When you walked in to Uwajimaya, you felt like you might be in Japan. It was unlike any other grocery store I had ever entered. It had huge tanks of live fish waiting to be picked by the shoppers, and it wasn't just lobster and crab but also weird-looking snapper and fish I had never heard of, much less cooked. Traveling to Uwajimaya was an experience for all the senses.

I wandered back into the family room.

"Why don't you guys come with me, and we'll get all the ingredients and make dinner for your dad on Sunday?"

"I'm supposed to meet up with Matt later today," Ash said.

I looked to Kate.

"Sure," she said. "I'll go."

One in. One out. This was becoming the pattern. Ash was a hard one to crack, but I didn't want to push. I sensed some real reluctance on his part to embrace any more than what he wanted to in this blended-family scenario. It was a wait-and-see game. But at the same time, it wasn't like I had wanted to do much with the adults in my life at his age.

So we dropped him off at his friend's house and headed to the Japanese grocery. And a good day it was, filled with laughter as we poked at funny-looking vegetables and tried to find all the foreign ingredients for our Father's Day meal.

On Sunday, I pulled out my knife and started cooking. We set the table in the solarium, added candles and flowers and a present from the kids and the kid-to-be, and toasted to Dad. This was a holiday I could deal with—no bad feelings and no worrying that I should be somewhere else. Just a celebration of the one guy who had brought this little group together.

"LET'S GET AWAY," I SAID with a matter-of-fact sigh a few weeks later in July. It was a bright morning as we sat looking out the windows over breakfast. My cold coffee sat on the table. I picked at the banana pancakes on the plate. "I need to get away. I think we all need to probably get away."

Art was reading the morning paper. It had been a difficult week at his clinic. It had been another tough week with Vicki and the kids. "Discussions" about finances, schedules, and more finances had, once again, been the theme for the week. We were both spent.

There was a claustrophobia that hung over us, our house, and this town. I felt it every morning. Despite our best efforts at moving on, it lingered like a bad smell. "What do you think?" I asked again.

He looked up. From our seats in the solarium, we watched the not-quite-grown-up chickens scatter around the flowerbeds. They shook their little yellow-and-red wings and tried scratching at the ground.

"I was thinking, since Ash is going to soccer camp in a week and you have Friday off, we might be able to head to Twisp for the weekend," I continued.

"We have Kate that weekend."

"I know. Maybe she'd like to go."

"Well, if you want to, sounds good to me," he said, as he stood and walked to the door with his cup of coffee. The cat head-butted his calf.

"Would you mind if I asked Kelly and Mary Jane?" I asked, skirting by him to walk outside by the little pond. "I haven't seen them in forever. It might be good to mix it up a little."

"Sure."

One week later, we locked the doors to the house, closed the trunk of the car, and settled in for the drive. My two girlfriends, whom I had known since junior high, were driving separately and would meet us later that evening at the cabin.

"All right, we're set," Art said to the air around us. "Let's go."

I got in the front seat and waited for the dragon breathing fire, sometimes known as Katherine, to clamber into the backseat. Tara, the old golden retriever, was panting hard in the way back, and Katherine had her Pomeranian puppy on her lap. We headed down the driveway, closed the gate, and decided on the music. The river was still pretty full with spring runoff, and the sun was out. We stopped for gas in Goldbar, a small town on Route 2, and grabbed some junky snacks for the drive.

"I think you'll like seeing my girlfriends again." I turned to Katherine, handing her a pep stick. "They're looking forward to hanging out with you."

Kate had met Mary Jane and Kelly at the wedding and had seen them a few times since then up at the house. I had seen her smile in amazement at their outrageous comments and potty humor.

I turned back toward the window. Katherine. Despite her spiked tongue and her continual challenge to my existence in this family picture, this blond, bold girl in the backseat had my heart, hook, line, and sinker. She exhausted me and my reserves of patience, but I regarded her strong feelings and her in-your-face attitude with a certain level of commendation. I wanted to see her relax and smile.

Almost the minute we hit the road, I felt some relief. A break in the action. After a quiet three-and-a-half-hour drive, we drove around the final bend. The sun was out, the black-and-white magpies gathered at the feeders, and a sense of reprieve descended. With a honk from the car, my girlfriends arrived in time for dinner. The fire-breather went away to her cave, and a truce of sorts occurred as I barbecued chicken and we all watched the sun go down between the knobby mountains out front.

Over the weekend, we went to the Methow River and wrangled rattlesnakes under the porch. Kate got to see me in my other world. The world with girlfriends who had known me forever and actually liked me. Friends who could tease me unmercifully about all the dumb stuff we had done growing up.

"Yes, we smoked!" they laughed out loud.

"Yes, we dined and dashed in that big, fat, white Cadillac," they howled.

"Yes, we couldn't hold it any longer, so we peed in the sink at the gas station," they screamed.

They laughed at my growing stomach. They poked fun at Art. It was such a gigantic relief to leave the arguments and disagreements in western Washington. For all of us. It wasn't often that Katherine was alone with us, without her brother. It allowed for more independent thoughts. She laughed. She watched all of us dance on the porch. She smiled and finally danced with us.

It was one of those weekends when I thought, *Okay, this will work itself out.* The refill button on my inner reserve tank turned on. Art and I still wanted the same things. That had not changed. The highway to get there was just going to be a little different than what I had expected. Expectations—they were really trying to crash the party.

*It hasn't even been a year yet,* I reminded myself. *We can do this!*

And as that beautiful baby kicked inside my stomach, I knew more than anything that I wanted to. I really wanted to. I loved this man. I had chosen this guy, this marriage, and this situation. I heard my dad describing women he admired: "She's a tough ol' broad." I could be that gal. I could do this.

FALL. NEW PENCILS AND PAPER. New clothes. New outlook on life. New couch to sit on as Art and I met with our first marriage counselor, Sally. One of Art's colleagues had recommended her to us. On her informational sheet, she listed blended families as a specialty area. She was also a stepmom. I sat there with Art next to me, separated by textured brown cushions. Looking at the lamp with the soft glow, the requisite box of tissues, the primary-color abstract painting behind her chair on the wall next to the door, I folded my hands on my stomach. I felt the baby kick.

Nodding and listening with little expression, she observed us as we told her the story of how we met and described how we fell in love. The Gottman approach to marriage counseling. Our stories were descriptive and similar. On the second visit, and with less enthusiasm, we described the past eleven months. Each subsequent week, we tried to discuss and understand the tensions, arguments, and discord that seemed to be taking up residence in our house.

Today, she looked at us and nodded.

"You are both really hurting."

*Yes*, I thought. *I know that already.*

It was only the fifth visit, but the immediate fix we both wanted was not looming on the horizon. These visits seemed merely to highlight the fact that we were both sad and frustrated. We sat there on that small brown sofa, both of us thinking about the money being spent during that hour and wondering if it was worth it. I looked at her skeptically when she mentioned with a laugh that there were many times when she got along better with her husband's first wife than she did with her husband.

So far, the only good thing to come out of these visits was the hour after, when we stopped in Seattle and had lunch, like the old days, grabbing at that memory of why we had come together in the first place. We were fighting less, talking more, but between my growing stomach and the millions of emotions, it was hard to know if this progress was lasting or temporary. All I wanted was to stop, have my man rub my expanding belly, and tell me it was going to be okay.

Sally was qualified, but counselors are a bit like a bra fitting: you think that lacy little number is going to be perfect, but it takes a while to find the right fit. And this one wasn't it. We stepped into her elevator after the ninth visit and looked at each other. We didn't go back.

"Let's make dates for lunch every week," he said. "That seems just as helpful to get us back on course."

"Mm-hmm," I murmured back in agreement.

He grabbed my hand, and we headed across the street, quiet in our thoughts. Ending our sessions with this counselor was the right decision, but it also felt a bit deflating. We had wanted more out of it—more complete answers to our questions on how to make a blended family work better than we seemed able to do at this point. I wanted answers that I optimistically thought were out there in the universe somewhere. But we weren't giving up the boat just yet. Lunches were a good idea. We had a baby coming. The sun was out. Seattle folks had their shades on. The leaves were gloriously orange. And the bacon burger with caramelized onions that we split tasted great.

"LOOK, THERE'S THE WHITE HOUSE," my older sister, Lolly, said enthusiastically to my mom and me.

In the fall of 1992, George H. W. Bush was the president and running for a second term against Governor Bill Clinton. Lolly, Mom, and me were in a taxi driving from National Airport to the Sulgrave Club. It was the first time I had been back to Washington, DC, in four years. I had gone to our nation's capitol in the fall of 1985, after I graduated from college, to start my political-science-bachelor-of-arts life. I had hoped to get a job on Capitol Hill, but my timing was off. The Gramm-Rudman-Hollings Act, legislation halting most new hires on the Hill, had just passed. I was lucky, though. After two months of interviews, I was offered and accepted a job with a private consulting and lobbying firm. I was the fourth hire and definitely the low woman on the totem pole, but I was excited and jumped right into this first real job.

I found a place to live in Georgetown. I memorized the route to work and walked there every day. I delivered information to the legislative offices on Capitol Hill, outlining our clients' interests and issues. I filed and typed up memos for the two principals in the firm. I washed the coffee cups at the end of the day.

I discovered that Washington, DC, is a good city to live in when you are single, poor, and a new hire in the political world. The museums are free, and so is the food at the various receptions held most evenings. There was an active nightlife with great music, great bars, and great people.

I took the Amtrak train to New York on the weekends to visit friends, listened to live music on the Mall, and traipsed through Maryland and Virginia.

I stayed in DC and worked at this firm for a little over two years. The company grew quickly, and I learned a lot about politics, personalities, and the pressurized bubble of being inside the Beltway. But there came a time when I had to decide either to stay for a long while or to move on. For one big reason and several small ones, I was ready to leave. I packed up my blue Volkswagen Golf and said goodbye to my friends. I drove one last time by the Mall, slowing to look at the Washington Monument and the Lincoln Memorial. I unrolled the front window and put my arm in the sun. Crosby, Stills, Nash, and Young sang from the speaker as I began my solo drive across the middle states of the country.

I was anxious to get home and back to the northwest. I was ready to help out my family. My brother Robert, second from the top, was sick.

MY MOM, LOLLY, AND I HAD arrived that morning in 1992 to see the AIDS quilt. The volunteers had already begun laying the blankets on the lawn, unfolding them at the base of the Washington Monument. The quilt was now roughly twenty-one thousand panels—the equivalent of almost fifteen football fields—and every one of them was going to be shown. Robert's panel was there, too. We had finished it on my parents' dining room table three years earlier. There, in that wood-paneled room, we had gathered—my mom and dad, my sister, my oldest brother, Minor, two of Robert's friends, and me—and each of us had sewn a memory.

The three of us had come a few days prior to the events of the quilt's unveiling to see the sights of the Capitol. We went to the memorials, Lincoln's and Vietnam's. We went to the museums. We had drinks at the rooftop bar overlooking the White House. We ran into some old friends and met some new ones. Coincidences were everywhere. One of our new friends was the call operator at the hospital where I was going to have my baby. My sister ran into old friends from Oregon. Art was arriving Friday night to see the quilt ceremony and attend a medical conference over the weekend, but those first few days were just the three of us.

Saturday morning, Mom, Lolly, and I stood on the podium, facing the quilt, and read thirty names from the panels before us. Then we read Robert's name together. We hugged each other. We hugged our new friends. We hugged strangers. We lingered for hours, looking at the quilt and feeling the unity of grief. There were so many emotions. That evening we lit candles and walked around the White House in a vigil with over three hundred thousand people. A male choir sang out to us as we passed, slowly, a mass of people turned into one entity.

When the ceremony was over, we all returned to the hotel and had a final nightcap to honor the weekend, our intertwined feelings of grief and love, and Robert.

It was a gift of sanctuary to be with my mom and sister those first few days. We got up early and snuggled into cozy white robes. We splurged on room service, read the paper, and in unison headed out into the city. It was just so easy.

I realized that I was searching for that same sense of warmth and silent understanding with my new family that I felt on this trip with my mom and sister. The comfortable silences. The ability to simply walk into a room and not feel like you have to say something. I recognized that I was feeling more and more like an outsider in that house on the hill.

Instead of a sense of solidarity, I felt isolation. I wanted us all to be in this together, unified in a feeling that we all wanted this family. Not just me. Not just their dad.

*But honestly,* I asked myself, *how could those two kids want it?* They liked the old family. Our counselor had told us that some schools of thought on blended families held that there is no such thing as a "second" family. Was there some truth in that? I wondered.

These kids had a family. Was I, as the stepmom, simply stepping into it?

It seemed as if some decisions were made weekly without my input—and yet these were decisions that affected me. I was drained from hearing all these decisions secondhand. Financial decisions. Kid decisions. Time decisions.

The back-and-forth between the kids and Art, and Art and me, was endless. We were like a bow tie, meeting in the middle to confront the Man and then heading back out to pace on our own sides. They sensed my irritation. It seemed impossible for Art to integrate all of us in his mind. He continued to separate us in his actions. Had I been naive going into this? Why did I wake up some days and simply want to run away?

THE MILESTONES OF OUR FIRST anniversary and my thirtieth birthday passed. My maternal instincts shifted into high gear, and I began nesting. I continued to put my imprint on the house. I painted and stenciled the baby's room. I made fires and lit candles. I set the ambience.

Our baby was due in January. "Please wait for Christmas to pass and your sister's birthday, and then you can come," I whispered to it, as I pulled into McDonald's to get my weekly eggnog shake, an indulgence I could not have predicted.

Finally, it was the last day of the year and some friends were coming for dinner. It was a rare-roast-beef-and-brussels-sprouts kind of night. I was not nostalgic for the end of 1992. The year had been significant, but "out with the old and in with the new" was what we all toasted to. I had much hope for 1993.

She arrived two weeks later at 2:10 a.m., after a week-night dinner of lamb chops and baked potato with my mom and dad. She was two weeks early and perfect. We presented her with Art's middle name, Marlowe.

She was born via C-section. In 1993, a C-section mom

with good insurance got to stay in the hospital for five days, capped by a steak-and-champagne dinner on the last night. I was not in any real big hurry to go back to the hill anyway.

Art stayed with us every night, sleeping on the pullout chair next to the window. My sister, my brother, my parents, my nieces, and my friends all came by to meet this new soul. My stepdaughter came with Art the second day. She smiled nervously and held her new sister gently. My stepson gave excuses, told his dad he was busy, and did not come all week.

ANTICIPATING, ADJUSTING, MOVING THINGS AROUND— this was what we had done for fifteen months, and when we brought home this brand-new member of this new family, we did it some more.

If people had shapes, like states have birds, my shape would be a circle. A circle of chairs. It is a circle of love, protection, some sadness, and lots of hope. No member's chair is ever removed. My brother's chair is still there. This circle easily expands and makes room for new members. It now had a new chair for this lovely baby girl, right next to the chairs of this family I had married fifteen months earlier.

# 6

## RUNNING LAPS

*M*Y STEPKIDS WERE NOW FULL-ON teenagers. Braces were being removed and driver's licenses were being issued. More time was being spent in the bathroom, trying new looks, and driving everywhere was still a major part of the day.

As we entered this second year of marriage, our relationships with each other continued to be complex. One day would be fraught with tension and tears; the next would be a mix of easygoing chatter and calm.

At fourteen, Katherine was still a presence not to be ignored. She laughed, screamed, cried, and joked. She was fun and energetic. She was a genius at finding new ways to argue on a continual basis. She tested me constantly. Despite the fact that I was the "adult," her jabs and slights were often painful.

Ashton grew taller and entered into his first romantic

relationships. He read constantly. He remained stoically quiet, and that was painful in its own way.

Art and I cajoled and coaxed. We played video games. We cheered for them at their sporting events. Art stayed up Saturday nights to watch *Saturday Night Live* and the local *Almost Live* show with them, finally creeping to bed at 2:00 a.m. I drove them up with their friends to Stevens Pass to ski and waited in line for hot chocolate. We listened and worried and talked constantly about these two kids. Wishing and hoping that the dividing line would go away and in its place a family would emerge.

"WE'RE SUPPOSED TO BE THERE at four-thirty," Katherine spoke hurriedly. "Red jerseys." She sat on the couch, talking on the phone, eating cantaloupe, and tying up her basketball shoes. "My mom said she could drive you home. You'll meet Doug. Her new boyfriend."

Are you eavesdropping when you're in the same room? I walked into the kitchen and turned, stifling the grin of huge relief that erupted from my face.

You would have thought I'd found cubes of gold bullion in the attic. Because even though my stepdaughter had told me expressly, "My mother told us she'll never get remarried until we graduate from high school," at least there was a body in the picture; Vicki and her friends had another person to sit with in the bleachers.

It was one more sign of forward movement. For the first six months of 1993, I carried on with an optimistic spirit. We all adapted to cries for food in the middle of the night and, without fail, the baby's need to nurse every single evening when we sat down to dinner. Katherine was learning to adjust to being a second daughter, and Ashton realized if he held that baby sister at soccer practice, it was equivalent to having a puppy—a magnet to get high school girls to come talk to him. We took little steps forward. We planned. We dreamed. We said, in our own, non-Biblical way, "All this shall pass."

There were days when I woke up with a small measure of excitement and less dread. We had this beautiful new baby who chattered away every day, and I was getting into the groove of communicating with my stepkids as stereotypical teenagers. I could judge by the amount of thudding on the steps whether this was going to be a morning to chat about dumb things or just keep quiet. I continued to relish my role as a mom of steps. And, despite missteps and stumbles, I think I was pretty good at it. I prepared homemade facial masks, and Katherine and I teased Ashton into smothering some on his face, too. We made ice-cream sundaes and sat on the couch, watching *Beverly Hills, 90210*. We popped popcorn and looked outside with excitement at the first snow falling. We drew scenes with paint on the windows with Katherine's first boyfriend in eighth grade. I introduced them to spicier tomato pasta, Swedish meatballs, French dip, tofu *bobotie*, and Swedish pancakes.

"You know, Mar, one good thing about having you here now?" Kate said to me one day in the car.

"What's that?" I asked.

"You're always on time!"

Even Ashton smiled at this conversation. All three of us laughed.

We traveled to Colorado for a medical meeting, hiked in the Rockies, and swam in the pool. We hired a babysitter, and the four of us experienced the exhilaration of rafting a big and fast river. We flew to North Carolina, where I experienced my first reunion as "the wife" with Art's family. We rode horses, barbecued, and hiked in the Smoky Mountains.

Those first months after the baby was born were really just about us. The five of us. Marlowe wasn't in daycare, Ash and Kate arrived every other day (and we spoke to them most days on the phone), my friends lived forty minutes or farther away, and nobody in town was inviting us over. And within the confines of us, it sometimes even clicked.

But, as is always the case, life marches on.

SUMMER ARRIVED AGAIN, AND I drove to meet my dad at the Dairy Queen in Woodinville, fifteen minutes south of us, to pick up the miscellaneous supplies that I would take to Twisp for the Fourth of July. Art, Marlowe, and I were headed over to the cabin with some old Seattle friends and then going to Canada for a short car-camping trip in the Bowron Lakes region.

My dad had his window rolled down when I drove into the parking lot. He smiled and did his half wave—a kind of half salute.

"Hey, Pops. Thanks for meeting me halfway. It saved us a lot of time." He seemed a little quiet, but I was in a hurry and didn't pay attention. I climbed back into the car.

"Have a great Fourth! Looks like the weather is going to be really nice."

"You have fun, too," he replied. "I'll talk to you when you get back."

We both waved and drove off.

Twisp was sunny and warm, and the seven of us had a good long weekend. On Tuesday, our friends returned home and Art and I started the laundry and went about the business of cleaning and closing up the cabin. We were set to leave the next day for Canada and excited for another road trip and Marlowe's first night in a tent.

Dad called in the afternoon. We chatted easily about the Fourth of July festivities. Then he said, "So, the doctor found something."

A pause.

"It looks like it's probably a tumor or something. We won't know more until later this week, when we get more results back from all the tests the doctors did."

Another pause.

"Oh, Dad." I sighed as I sat down on the back step. I looked at the deer coming down the hill behind the cabin.

"I don't want you to come home. Take your camping trip, and by the time you get back, we'll have more answers."

I talked to my mom and then again to my dad.

"I love you, Pops. We'll get through this."

MY DAD WAS DIAGNOSED WITH liver cancer. He had never been a big drinker, and the doctors had little explanation for us. Perhaps it was the chemicals from the printing presses where he had worked in sales most of his life, or even his early exposure to bombing tests while serving on a naval carrier during the Korean War. But those details didn't matter. It was cancer, and not a good kind.

The diagnosis took my whole family by surprise. Since my brother's death, we had cared for and buried both of my mom's parents also. And after three deaths in short order, you begin to think that, with any luck, you are kind of done with funerals for a while. My mom, sister, brother, and I had all started putting back together the pieces of our individual lives, but within moments we collectively did a U-turn and went back into caregiver mode.

My dad was sixty-six and had just retired several months earlier. A pain in his gut had sent him to see his doctor, and the subsequent oncologists were less than optimistic.

"Maybe six months," the doctor somberly said.

After exhaustively talking to everyone around the country, Art found an alternative treatment being used by a doctor in Camden, New Jersey. My dad decided to try it. That fall of 1993, my mom and dad, Art, the baby, and I packed our bags and all traveled there. Camden: home of Campbell's soup and, at the time, not much else. Art stayed for the initial consultation and then returned home. We had agreed that Marlowe and I would stay with my mom and dad for the six weeks during which the protocols would be undertaken and delivered into my dad's body.

On his non-treatment days, we traveled to Gettysburg and Amish country. We toured Ben Franklin's home and saw the Liberty Bell. The doctor was brilliant and eccentric. His office lay in the deep depths of a decaying hospital that felt as sick as the patients within. Walking through those hallways felt like a strange, futuristic movie without the music. The motel we stayed in had three locks on the door—a testament to the environment in the streets outside. Every night we locked the doors and prepared our weird motel dinner in the small kitchenette. We marveled at the intelligence of my nine-month-old baby as she picked the red square or the yellow circle and put them in the right place on top of the toy bucket.

"She must be the smartest baby ever!" we laughed.

The next morning, we would unlock that door and enter the day with hope and worry and faked enthusiasm.

Six weeks went by. This experimental treatment ended, to be followed up back in Seattle with a chemotherapy protocol and patience. My dad would not know the results of the experimental drugs for another month.

We were all ready to get home and back to some semblance of our old routines. I missed Art. I missed Katherine and Ashton. I was ready to wear some other clothes and shower in my own bathroom.

But during the six weeks that I had been gone, I had not talked with Ashton or Katherine very much, and upon my return, our conversation was strained. They were not sure what to say or how to act. I didn't blame them one bit. They were just beginning to get to know my dad and, like so much of this blended-family reality, the relationship was too early for deep feelings one way or another.

Just as I did not know their family histories, they didn't know mine, either. And as teenagers, they weren't too inclined to want to know. They knew I could cry at Kodak commercials, but they had not really seen me shed tears from true sadness. They knew I sometimes said off-color things when I called people on the phone—"Are you naked?"—but they had not experienced the seriousness with which I advocated for sensitivity and generosity toward my family and friends.

I worried about my mom, and I ached for my dad. He was in my thoughts every hour of the day. He had had many plans for retirement and he was angry about his predicament. Soon after returning home, he started chemotherapy and tried to get back to his life. My brother, sister, and I went home to help him and my mom as often as we could. We talked. We laughed. We cried. And we all crossed our fingers and prayed for the best.

I LOOKED OUT THE CAR window toward the high school. I was distracted with everything going on, but the rush of high-schoolers always intrigued me: their subtle rituals, awkward shrugs, and general self-consciousness. It was October, and I was parked in my usual spot for after-school pickup, the parking lot of the diner where I had first met Katherine and Ashton. Our next stop was the orthodontist.

Kate appeared from the teenage masses, practically skipping, her ponytail bouncing with each step.

She pulled open the door.

"I got asked to the prom!" she exclaimed with a huge smile. She closed the door and put on her seat belt. She was literally shaking with delight. Her left knee bounced up and down. She flipped the radio station and waved to someone as we pulled out of the parking spot.

"This is so great!" she exclaimed, grabbing for the water bottle I had left for her in the cup holder.

Her excitement was so overwhelming, so genuine and full. It was contagious—I felt like I had been invited to the prom, too.

"He came up to me after lunch when I was walking back to my locker," she continued, telling me about the big ask.

*God*, I thought. *You're growing up. . . .*


KATHERINE. YOU WERE IN-BETWEEN when I first met you that New Year's weekend. Still a little girl on some days and a ready-to-explode teenager on others. Your face expressed so many emotions. You had that shiny-eyed, big-smile, little-girl excitement at birds and bugs and puppies, but it also held a shadow of self-conscious awkwardness and a hint of future pissiness and sass. You were skinny and athletic, with blondish-brown hair still searching for a good haircut.

Eyes. You had eyes that looked at everything. They peered around corners, threw lasers from the backseat of the car, and watched from your upstairs bedroom window, which opened up over our kitchen. They were like ears—observing and listening.

Before your dad and I got married, I tried to share with you my excitement for our wedding. I told you about the food—lamb chops—and the band. My mom and I took you to the Laura Ashley shop adjoining the Four Seasons in Seattle to try on the black velvet dress with the white lace collar that you would wear as a member of my black-and-white-themed wedding party. The days were very rushed that October week before the wedding. Your aunt and uncles arrived and stayed with you at our house with so little furniture. I hugged you after the ceremony and hoped you would dance. Later, I heard you cried—really hard—when we left the reception as a married couple.

You were then, and are now, your daddy's girl. And you are your mom's girl.

Some days, in that first year, I felt like you were staring at me as if I were from a different country. I didn't dress like the people you knew. I ate different foods. I drank wine with dinner. Every once in a while, for shock value or simply to break the tension and make people laugh, I would holler with a smile, "This situation calls for one thing—a good old shout of 'motherfucker'!"

Your mouth opened wide when you saw me smoking that one and only cigarette with my old high school girl-friends on the front deck of the house as you watched from the upstairs bedroom window. You fluctuated between nervous chatter, a teensy bit of admiration, and genuine wonder: *What is she doing here?*

You were, and continue to be, loud.

You kicked shoes and slammed bathroom doors. You yelled for your brother to get the phone and screamed in frustration at your dad for not explaining algebra problems in a way you could understand.

You cried. For yourself. For your mom. For this situation. You cried in anger and in sadness. You cried on the phone. You cried in bed.

On the mornings that you were at our house, you would tromp down the back stairs, through the office and the family room, and into the kitchen to see what was for breakfast.

In the beginning, I put out everything—napkins, bowls,

and utensils all lined up next to cereal, muffins, toast, fruit. It must have felt like a bed-and-breakfast. I could tell the minute I saw your face whether it was a morning for conversation or not. That first year, it was mostly not.

Eventually, I learned what you liked for breakfast. Cantaloupe was always a favorite. So, even though I knew you could figure out your own breakfast, I put out cantaloupe, sliced and ready to eat. I put out cereal. I made oatmeal on cold days. I thought it was important for you to wake up and know someone was thinking about you.

Back then, I silently prayed you would not get your first period at my house. I turned magazine pages trying to figure out how to make your bedroom a bedroom and not a rest stop. I woke up every day thinking about what to make for dinner. Something that you and your brother would eat and enjoy. You loved mustard crumbed chicken with parsley and rice.

"WILL YOU TAKE US SHOPPING for the prom dress, Mar? Brittney and Nicole were asked today, too. We all want to go together to shop."

She was talking fast about everything that circled around the word *prom*. The dress. The hair. The makeup. Some strip-mall store in Lynnwood that she and her girlfriends had heard was the best place to get dresses.

"Sure," I said, immediately wondering what her mom would think. "When do you all want to go?"

The following week, I drove down to the gym and picked up her and her two girlfriends from basketball practice and drove to the dress store. Marlowe smiled in back amid all the attention. This store screamed, *Prom!* from the parking lot. It had everything. Every color. Every mood. Demure to slutty styles. Beads. Bangles. Silk. Chiffon. But we found it. A long, dark blue velvet dress. It was elegant, with a turtleneck halter top. She looked fabulous, even if she had just come from practice. It cost more than her parents had budgeted. I bought it anyway.

"So, who are you asking?" we both asked Ashton that night after shopping. He was newly single, mopey, and missing his old girlfriend.

"I don't know," he mumbled.

"C'mon, you have to invite someone—it's your senior year! It's homecoming!" Katherine poked at him.

"Well, I may invite Shelley. Her sister is going with Lucas, and then maybe we'll all go as a group."

ASHTON. YOU WERE NOT IN-BETWEEN when we met. You were on the cusp. You were tall, slim, and strong, with bushy, dark eyebrows and blond hair. You had a beautiful smile. You were sensitive. When we first met, I watched you unself-consciously hold your dad's hand. I hadn't seen a teenage boy do that. I thought it was sweet.

Starting that first weekend in Twisp, you seemed always to have a book in your hand. Science fiction, mystery, or suspense. *Dune, Andromeda Strain, The Bourne Ultimatum.*

You played a lot of Sega and tried to teach me the moves.

From the beginning, you were more detached than your sister. You sat back and watched. Sometimes you were in the house but not really there. You were very quiet and solemn.

Early on after the wedding, I took you shopping for shoes at Nordstrom. The sales clerk asked if I was your sister. We were both embarrassed.

I knew you were smart. You were an achiever. Straight A's. Band. Soccer. Student government. Your schedule was mind-boggling.

I had never seen a high school kid throw the soccer ball in from the sideline the way you did. Down the sideline you would run, and in one swift movement execute a front flip and hurl the ball out to your team. You could throw the ball almost half the field.

If a person can be open and closed at the same time, you were. You tolerated Katherine and me as we teased you about your girlfriends. You were not enthusiastic about helping with the firewood. You pestered the cats. You avoided conflict.

"HOW'S IT GOING?" I ASKED. Ashton was sitting on the couch, legs splayed, watching television. A spiral tablet lay on his knees.

"I don't know. Okay, I guess. These questions are stupid."

College applications and information were stacked on the coffee table at his side.

"Well, let me know if you want me to read 'em. I used to be kind of good at those types of essays," I said, trying hard to be light and humorous, as I walked through the family room. "Which question are you working on?" I asked.

"My interests."

"What are the other ones?"

"Describe a significant event and its impact on you. Name a favorite book character and why."

"Mmm," I said. "How far along are you?"

"Not very."

I went into the kitchen. It was cold out that day. Winter was definitely in the air.

"How does chili and cornbread sound tonight?" I asked him. I heard a grunt from the couch.

I pulled out the meat and started chopping the onions.

"DO WE HAVE ANY HONEY for the cornbread?" Katherine asked that night.

"Yeah. It's on the shelf, next to the peanut butter."

"Why don't you write about your experience going to Holland with your soccer team?" Art asked Ashton.

"Yeah, maybe."

A couple of days later, he was on the couch again. "Any progress?" I asked.

"A little."

"C'mon, let me read it," I kidded. "I told you I would type it up. I'm going to have to read it then anyway."

He passed it over, and for the next couple of weeks, he and I went over the drafts. His interests and his significant event. Soccer and science. His parents' divorce.

By the time we had finished, he had written some smart, amazing essays. And that space of hours working with him on them was huge for me. He called me "Mar."

Conversation between Ashton and me had been hit or

miss at times since I'd married Art. As he opened up, wrote things down, and let me read and suggest, I experienced a welcome surprise: the walls of resistance had come down a little; he had let me into his private world. I relished it like a kid eating her favorite candy.

"Ashton has a date for the prom," Katherine tattled at the table a few nights later.

"All right!" Art replied. "Who's the lucky girl?"

Later that night, listening to the kids chattering about the prom events, I turned to Ashton and said, "Hey, why don't you and your friends have dinner over here before the dance? I'd be happy to make something," I continued, warming up to this idea. "You know, it would make it a lot cheaper for you guys. We could do fondue, you know, with the meat and all the different mustards and sauces." I looked at him. "Fondue is fun. If the conversation goes slowly, you have something to do."

The menu was set. Fondue, barley and pine nuts, and a simple green salad with ranch dressing. Martinelli's cider.

The weekend before the prom, Art and I were getting ready to sit down for a movie and dinner. Clam chowder simmered on the stove, and bread was in the oven. The baby was in bed; the fire was lit and roaring behind the glass doors of the Russian fireplace. The kids were at Vicki's for the weekend. It was a good evening. But I had been thinking about the prom at our house the following weekend. Our weekend.

It was going to be a full house up on the hill for that homecoming prom on a fall evening in the Northwest. Katherine and her girlfriends were going to get ready upstairs before their dates picked them up and took them to a local restaurant for dinner. Ashton and his group of ten were arriving at five-thirty for pictures before the fondue dinner. I was excited and happy to be part of the mix. It was a good distraction from my dad's illness.

I looked at Art as he ladled some clam chowder into his bowl.

"I think we probably should ask Vicki if she wants to come up next weekend for the prom night. All the girls are getting dressed here before they go to dinner," I said. "And Ashton's whole group will be here, too."

He looked up at me. We had just gotten over a major brouhaha with her when we had received a subpoena from her attorney on Art's birthday. Her attorney was continuing to nitpick over our attempt to refinance our home. We still needed Vicki to sign off on it because of the lien she had on the property. With big words and a hint of threat, the subpoena was to verify that we were not trying to get rid of the lien. Vicki had said she hadn't known it would arrive on that day, but the whole episode stung. I had been home with the kids, making a double-chocolate birthday cake, when I had opened the door and received the package. Then my dad randomly called and I broke down in tired sobs as he held me up over the phone lines. The kids sat uncomfortably in the family room.

Art looked back at me. "Do Katherine and Ash want her to come up?"

"I haven't talked to them about it. I was just thinking about it today."

It was Kate's first prom. I sure as heck would want to be

there to see all the girls get dressed at my daughter's first prom, so I called.

"Hi, Vicki. It's Marianne."

She gave me her usual curt response: "Hi. What's up?"

"Well, I'm sure the kids told you about the plans for prom night next week ... I was wondering if you wanted to come up and help them get dressed and be a part of the whole thing."

She did want to.

I listened to Vicki, Kate, and her friends laughing and talking as I made dinner downstairs. Vicki had been polite but reserved and a bit prickly when she arrived. Shortly, the doorbell rang and I watched Art shake hands with Kate's date and invite him into the family room.

I heard familiar footsteps down the back stairs and looked up as Kate walked into the room with her mom. Kate shone. We all laughed as this awkward kid put on her wrist corsage and as Kate struggled to pin on his boutonniere. Pictures were taken, of Kate and Art, Kate and Vicki, Kate and her date.

Ashton's group arrived, and more pictures were shot. With giggles and clicking heels, we all said goodbye and the first group of friends left the house for the night's activities.

We could hear Ashton and his friends laughing in the dining room while we all sat in the kitchen. The fondue seemed successful. My sister was watching Marlowe at her house, so the three of us sat down and talked about the upcoming schedule and the holidays. We chatted about the kids.

The dinner was over quickly, Ash's friends said goodbye and thank you, and—swish—they were gone.

"Have fun tonight!" we all said in unison. "Drive safe!"

"Well, I guess I'll get going, too," Vicki said, picking up her purse.

"Okay," I replied.

Art closed the door behind her. I was spent. I know it was my house and my effort, and the evening had seemed fairly successful. But it was also one of those nights when I felt invisible, lost in the background, an addendum. That feeling drained me.

I cleared the plates from the dining table and started the dishes. I blew out the candles. Art let the dogs outside one last time. We turned off the kitchen lights and went to bed, tired.

MY DAD WAS FEELING PRETTY good, considering the wear and tear on his body and mind from all the chemicals, doctors, and not-always-positive news. And that fall, my parents decided to take us all on a vacation. We got through the holidays, and in February 1994, they flew the entire family—twelve of us—to Maui. My five gathered for our first family photograph in front of the Hawaiian sunset with the baby in the middle.

The vacation was a mix of every emotion that poets and writers have ever described. It was sunny and beautiful and smelled good. We all rallied to make each day joyful. But I felt pulled in many directions. Katherine and Ashton had never spent day after day with my family, and it was sometimes awkward. My sister's children were young, and my brother did not have kids. Teenagers of any sort were a bit of a puzzle to them, and they, too, had not spent day after day with Ash and Kate. Everyone was getting to know each other in a new and different way.

Plus, my siblings and I were struggling with the emotions of losing our dad. Would this be our last vacation with him?

Interactions on all sides fluctuated. Sometimes my siblings tried too hard and it didn't work. Other times, a real connection was made, a moment to remember.

Kate and Ash were all over the place. They were sometimes shy and quiet and hid behind books and magazines. Other moments, they laughed with genuine feeling and spontaneity. We swam and snorkeled and ventured out past Makena beach on the lava trail. Ash stole looks at the nude beach, and Kate snorkeled with her dad.

"It meant a lot to me that you guys came on this trip," I said to them both as we sat on the beach, looking for the green spot in the sunset, on our last night on Maui.

"I know this isn't always easy. But the trip wouldn't have been the same for me if you hadn't come."

The ocean reflected the end of the day. We all sat and watched the sun go down.

We were quiet as we pulled into the driveway of their mom's home after we landed at the airport. Art got out of the car to help them take their suitcases inside. I hugged Ash and then Kate. I didn't grow up in a family that said, "I love you" much out loud; we said it in cards on birthdays, and in letters we wrote from camp and college. Expressing it out loud, especially to Katherine and Ashton, was not yet in my comfort zone. I'd written it out and even mumbled it a few times. But the trip, my dad, and everything we had been through in this first year of holidays, summer vacation, and sporting events welled up inside me.

"We'll see you guys in a couple of days," I said. "I love you."

I didn't expect an answer, and I didn't get one. That wasn't the point. It was just time.

We all marched on.

Months later, on a partially cloudy Friday afternoon in May, I left the house on the hill with Marlowe to drive to Everett and pick up Art from work. It was Memorial Day weekend. We were headed to Twisp to meet up with my folks and do the annual spring cleanup. I watched him walk through the parking lot to the car, and I knew something had happened; I assumed it had been just another day at the office, where backstabbing, egos, and attitudes clashed.

He opened the door and sat down in the passenger seat. He closed the door. "They fired me."

"What do you mean?" I looked at him. It's true that your stomach clenches and feels like it plunges downward. Your palms go cold. Your hair follicles tingle a little. Bad news does that—especially when it is shocking news that was nowhere in your line of sight. You don't know the vocabulary. The language is foreign. They don't teach this jargon in college.

We sat there in the parking lot, shocked into silence. The baby babbled happily in back. The dogs looked up from the rear. We looked at each other, and then we looked straight ahead, out the front window.

"Let's go," he said impulsively. "Let's just go to Twisp."

I started the car and drove out of the parking lot. It was

pure habit. Muscle memory kicked in: use the blinker, tap the brakes, press the gas pedal. We drove through the stoplights, turning left toward the on-ramp. We headed north, up Interstate 5, as if things were normal and we were going away for the weekend. Ha. We made it about five miles before I called my folks and we turned around for the house on the hill.

In a daze, we made dinner and put the baby to bed. He told me the details of the afternoon. The closed door. The conversation. The lack of looks from the other employees, people he had known and worked with for a long time.

We went over and over and over every part of each sentence and utterance out loud and in our heads. The situation—a dynamic involving three partners—at his clinic had been strained for many months, but, after numerous meetings with the board and the other decision makers, we had felt secure in Art's future at the clinic.

We were flattened. The air was gone. We went to bed and tried to sleep.

At some point in that nighttime despair, Art's nature kicked in. He is a doer, a face-the-facts kind of guy. He was up at 4:00 a.m., and by Sunday night he had outlined a business plan to start his own practice.

Telling Ashton and Katherine was difficult. Even though you do not have any reason to be, you feel humbled and a little embarrassed. After the hurt of their parents' marriage ending and the gossip surrounding the divorce and Art's remarriage to me, the words "Dad was fired" felt like we were putting one more block on their shoulders.

Ashton was headed to college in the fall, and we assured him this would not change anything, although both Art and I had already brought it up between ourselves over the weekend and were both silently a little worried about it. Katherine, for once, didn't have much to say at all.

"Everything is going to be fine," Art told them. "This will probably end up being a good thing." He smiled.

They gave him self-conscious hugs and looked at me.

Within a week, we had gotten a business license, hired a nurse, and opened the doors to our new practice on Colby Avenue in Everett, two blocks from his former employer. Art would do the medical part; I would try to do everything else. It was a slow and challenging start. We stumbled over each other as I found child care, rented furniture, and ordered supplies for the office. Art had lengthy conversations with his former office to negotiate a retrieval of phone numbers and addresses of his old patients in order to contact them and tell them where we were now located. I turned on my computer and formulated spreadsheets. I scrambled to educate myself on how to bill insurance companies, learning health billing codes, filing and payroll-deduction instructions, and state tax laws regarding small businesses. I raised my eyes to the gods and hoped I was doing it right. We met with attorneys about our plans and options. Our learning curve was very steep, and our patience was tested daily.

We enlisted Ashton to man the front desk. We called and contacted as many of Art's former patients as we could, but their health issues could not always wait for us and Art lost many of his longtime clients.

These events tested our tolerance. Our emotions ran high and were quickly triggered as we staggered through the next months in our new "normal."

It was a time when solo practitioners were going out of business and becoming a rarity. We tried to fight our doubts and push ahead with enthusiasm, but we were both nervous and concerned.

By the end of that year, our income had dropped 75 percent from the previous year.

THESE EVENTS—ILLNESS, WORK ISSUES, finances, and mere day-to-day existence—are life. But my new family was only beginning its second year, and this potent combination proved to be quite the stew.

Despite the hurdles that we had clambered over and the positive steps we had accomplished, our foundation was not fully set. We were not fully prepared as a united front for life's inevitable obstacles. So, instead of circling the wagons and binding together, we operated as single units. Yes, we dished out a lot of hugs, but by and large the bigger fears and anxieties were left to each person to hold and swallow on their own. There was not enough time in the day or sufficient energy in any of us to feel the weight of all of this as one entity.

The kids had an out—every other day, they went to the other house and could avoid the realities of life at our home. I think they were often very relieved to go back to their mom's. Our house was being rocked by outside stuff that was hard, even for their dad and me. Often we found ourselves having another "family meeting" to keep them in the loop on the latest obstacle, or we avoided the subjects altogether because it felt like an attack on them.

To describe it as hard does not do it justice. Internally, I was reeling—scared and frozen one moment, agile and ready for action the next. Externally, I put on a happy face and when asked, "How are you?" I smiled, but I never, ever gave an honest, gut-wrenching answer.

IN LATE AUGUST, ART AND I drove Ashton to college in California, unpacked his belongings, and experienced the multiple emotions surrounding the first child's leaving home. Ashton was so excited to be at college. He melded into the freshman crowd as if he had been there for weeks. Art experienced a mixture of pride in his son's accomplishments, the gratification of knowing his son was on a good path, and knowledge of the fact that eighteen years had gone by—as quickly as everyone says they do—and that the next chapter in the relationship with his child was an unopened book.

My three-year window with Ash when we all lived together in the same house was over. I hoped that whatever hoops we had jumped through were enough for me to sustain a continued relationship with him.

Back at home, Katherine had to adjust to being without her brother as a buffer. Maturity—I mean high school—had given her some new outlets, good ones and bad ones. It was difficult to know whether her choices and her vocabulary were a lingering result of the divorce or typical high-school-girl pushback. Both houses had different rules about similar things—how late boys could stay, weekend curfews, and non-curricular activities—and she was able to use those differences to her benefit. She would stay at the house that had the rule that worked best for her and her activities. She continued to yell and scream. She was angry, unhappy, and full of spite. Art and Vicki were on the phone a lot. Kate and I hit a new high level of arguing and disagreeing. We all decided to attend family counseling. I was the first one to arrive, and I paused before I sat down, finally picking a solo chair, so Art and Vicki could sit together on the couch, as her parents.

MY DAD CONTINUED CANCER TREATMENTS and surpassed the doctor's original six-month estimate, but by Thanksgiving his body had had enough. My dad was a sensitive and kind man. He was also a man who didn't waste words. He was aware of many of the struggles in my family, including the angst and aggravation that Kate and I had thrown at each other. I drove her down a week before he died, and he took a look at both of us and, with all the kindness and firmness that only a dying man knows, told Kate and me to "get our act together." Kate smiled, a little uncomfortable with the words and the situation. I nudged her with my arm in comradeship, letting her know not to worry.

"We will, Dad."

I smiled at him. Only my dad could cut to the chase and speak to the heart of the matter in such a fine way.

He died in his bed at home in the middle of the night, days before Thanksgiving. I walked with Ashton and Katherine down the aisle of the neighborhood Episcopal church. Art carried Marlowe. My family all sat in the pew. They watched as my sister, brother, and I each eulogized our dad. It was their first funeral.

WHEN MARLOWE TURNED TWO, WE enrolled her in the local Montessori school. She was ready for more socialization, and so was I. This school, located in the old part of town, was still headed up by the very same administrators that Ashton and Katherine had had many years ago when they had attended the same school.

I loved this place. From the very first day, when I lied about Marlowe being completely potty-trained, these amazing people accepted me as Marianne. It was a gift, to say the least.

I loved driving there, dropping Marlowe off, and watching her wave goodbye as the teacher held her hand. I loved volunteering in the classroom. It was filled with the pure, honest joy that small people project. Little preschoolers don't give you the stink-eye or the cold shoulder. They laughed and acted silly, and we all giggled together.

But that darn community! A lot of people were still shunning or avoiding us, and this environment was the perfect mix of ingredients to create anxiety and paranoia.

When it comes right down to it, we all want to belong to a community. Be a member. Feel like part of the pack, part of the structure. Membership is like a compass point. It gives you a direction and balance. When all else falls apart in the day, it's nice to sit back and know you are still part of something besides the immediate mayhem around you. My attempts to be part of the community made me feel, at times, as if I were attempting to climb a sand dune. My thighs felt the burn, but the inner goddess kicked in and, slipping and sliding, with a lift of the chin, I attempted to keep hiking up.

I had been reaching out to people for many, many months. I invited them for dinner, had casual conversations at the gym, and went out for coffee.

I reached out to the folks who made sense. People I had gone to college with or had some weird connection to from the past. People I had been introduced to at the holiday office party—the usual suspects, individuals and couples, whom you look for when you move to a new place. And Art had lost pretty much all of his old friends, so, in many respects, we were both starting from scratch.

I barbecued ribs and made salmon with garlic-citrus sauce. We broke bread and poured wine and water. We hosted holiday parties and weekend dinners. But my initial attempts at social connection were met with indifference and cold air. The town had not grown in population very much, and it seemed as if even the people I was reaching out to had some connection to Art's previous life there. They were not interested. The phone rang, but it rang for my stepdaughter to babysit for them, or they called to solicit donations to the latest local charitable cause. My membership card in this community was proving to be more of an uphill battle than I ever could have imagined.

I got lonely. And with each month, my loneliness was becoming more acute and painful. After all the draining life events I had experienced, combined with my isolation and the uncertainty of our new business and financial future, I felt alone in a room with no window.

The important relationships in my life—with my step-kids, and with Art—were still sputtering. I quickly discovered that talking to Ashton on the phone while he was in college was going to be even more difficult than talking to him in person. By the time the phone was passed to me, he had told his dad pretty much everything he wanted to share about his life, and we found ourselves making small talk—an exercise I think we both found draining.

Kate and I, well, we were still complicated. I remembered a childhood pull-tab book of Dr. Doolittle that I grew up with and that featured a two-headed llama. When you pulled the tab, the heads went back and forth, one side trying to pull, the other pushing, and then back again. It reminded me of us.

She confided in me, sharing deep secrets. She railed against me for trying to make rules when I was not her "real" mother. I tried to support her when she floundered. I expressed irritation and anger at her lack of respect. We pushed. We pulled.

Art and I were constantly "trying." Trying to get ahead of the boulder that seemed to be right behind us, threatening to knock us off our feet. If it was just the two of us, we could usually maneuver around and wiggle our way back to the love that had brought us together. But parenting is tough, and step-parenting is tougher. We often disagreed on what to do and how to go about it. Sometimes I wanted to be tougher than he did. Sometimes I thought his discipline was too tough. We were both tired of talking with Vicki about the different rules that we all used in the tug-of-war between us. Our disagreements made us feel isolated and alone.

WHEN ART AND I MARRIED, I did not have any friends who were stepparents. In fact, the majority of my closest friends did not have any kids at all. Understandably, my friends got tired of my talking about the whole blended-family situation.

I wanted someone to talk to, but I needed someone who got it, someone who could help me understood the ins and outs of being a stepmom. What steps was I missing? What did I not understand about this complicated, twisted relationship? It seemed logical that if I could figure out the most difficult part of this marriage—step-parenting—then the other parts might work better, too.

There was no Google or Bing in the mid-1990s, no fast and easy way to research resources. But there were free newspapers with advertisements for parent groups on the back pages. One for blended families caught my eye. Optimistically (hi ho, hi ho), I stepped into the counseling world again.

This woman was a better fit. Jane had become a counselor for blended families after years of being a stepmom herself. I liked her from day one. She knew without a ton of explanation when I described how I felt as if I were living with the Mother, too. She nodded knowingly when I voiced my exasperation at my stepdaughter's backtalk and frustration at my stepson's quiet stone face. She knew the facts on the marriage survival rate (not real good) of blended families.

I had been seeing her for a couple of months when she invited me to join a stepmom group she was putting together. It was a small group, and step-parenting was pretty much all we had in common, but it was fascinating. Some of us had very young stepkids; others, like mine, were teenagers. To no one's surprise, we all had issues with our spouses. All of our husbands thought we were overreacting, or they did not want to talk about it anymore, or they were angry, and on and on. We all had very strong opinions—good and bad—about our spouses' ex-wives.

But one thing stood out. Our families were now the broken ones. We had all gotten married to have our own family, but that family we had all looked forward to now felt like a jagged rock quarry. Cold. Hard. Stuck. Trying to assimilate our husbands' children into some kind of whole was a full-time role with no mentor and no job description.

Some of these moms saw their husband's children only sporadically, every other weekend or one day a week, or on holidays. They didn't have enough time to relate to anything, much less a child. There was a constant low hum in the room, an unarticulated whisper: *This would be easier if the child simply stayed at the other home.* The child did not like us. There was tension when the child was there. The other home was so horrible that when the child arrived, there was simply no chance of having normal, calm interactions. We all had a common theme of bickering over schedules, money, manners, and lack of respect.

All of us were in the first years of our relationships and were extremely tired. I am not sure whether our mutual fatigue helped or hurt us. On the one hand, we had all entered these marriages with excitement and anticipation; on the other hand, we had folks in the relationship who were not really excited about us being there: the ex-spouses, the communities, the kids. In some respects, the fatigue simply masked our feelings of failure: failure in our relationships, failure as moms, failure in ourselves.

I think the failure of our group to help also felt like a failure overload, as we petered out.

All we seemed to be saying to each other were mere words, simple clichés that did nothing. The concepts of simply hanging in there, letting more time go by, just waiting it out were frustrating in their lack of concrete action items. Our dreams were muddled. Our stepchildren were not puppies we could train to come at a whistle, and the inner workings of our individual relationships were not what we had planned. Do-overs were needed, but so was some help and support.

We were all alone on the teeter-totter.

THOSE FIRST YEARS WERE A mix of thick fog and sunlight. If I drew a picture of what I felt like I was doing every day, it would be a picture of several of me, running parallel around a track. One of me would be thinking about my stepdaughter, how to make her more comfortable, more full of smiles. One of me would be thinking about my stepson, how to break through to him, to convince him I care. One of me would be thinking of my husband, wondering how to get back our spark and sense of humor. One of me would be playing with my daughter, laughing and smiling. There were other thoughts on that track—the mother, the folks in the community, my mom—but we, all of the me's, kept going around that track.

Once in a while, I will admit, I looked for the exit—the place where I could get off and run in a different direction. Really fast.

But, usually, at that crucial moment, one of them would look at me—his sorry but solid green eyes, or her old-soul, sparkly ones, or even the dark, afraid-to-trust ones—and I'd take a deep breath and do another lap.

# 7

❧

# OUR FAMILIES (MINE)

$\mathcal{O}$UR MERGER INCLUDED OUR EXTENDED families. Mine. My husband's. And hers—the Mother's. They are a slice of my story as a stepmom.

My mom and dad were native Seattleites. They married in 1955 and had four kids in seven years, two boys and two girls. I am the youngest. We grew up across the lake from Seattle in what is now the fourth-largest city in Washington State, but in the 1960s and 1970s, it felt like a small town. We had chickens and dogs, ducks and lambs. In the summers, my mom threw us out of the house and told us not to come back until we heard the cowbell ring for dinner. We played kickball in the Wheelers' driveway and capture-the-flag in the woods above the Cowles's house with all the local neighbor kids. I had aunts and uncles and cousins everywhere.

We all went away for college and jobs, but eventually all

four of us returned to the Northwest, the land of lakes and mountains and, for those of us who grew up with *Here Come the Brides* and Bobby Sherman, the most beautiful skies you've ever seen.

My brother Robert had barely whispered to us that he was gay before he was diagnosed with HIV/AIDS. It was 1987, and in our small corner of the world, AIDS was one scary topic and hard to talk about outside our family group. Its causes and conditions were still mostly unknown and greatly exaggerated.

His illness became known to Mom, Dad, my siblings, and me following the evening of my grandmother's eightieth birthday, when three generations had gathered at the Columbia Tower Club to eat and celebrate Grandmother Helen. After the party, he ended up in the emergency room and called our other brother, Minor, for help the next morning. I had already caught my flight back to Washington, DC, and found out he was ill only when I arrived at my apartment.

From that early November evening on, his body fought a losing battle that lasted a short thirteen months.

Robert's illness was a remarkable and significant experience for my parents, my siblings, and me. When I pulled into the familiar driveway of my childhood home after leaving Washington, DC, Robert had already moved back in. He never left again. Between our drives in the car to his various doctors, our walks with his dog, Grey, through our old neighborhood, and the laughter at dinner that brought us all to tears, we created a deep, deep bond between us. Counselors will tell you these hardships can drive a wedge between family members; in our case, it cemented us pretty tightly. In the final months, we knew each other more intimately, both physically and emotionally, than we ever had before. We rubbed his feet with lotion, we bathed him, and we applied Vaseline to his chapped lips. We experienced the magical mystery of the final hours before he died.

This real-life event influenced the direction of our lives and futures. I was much more open to meeting and marrying Art because of my brother's death. As I said before, it provided a clear picture that there were no guarantees, that life can be fleeting, and that love and happiness should be grabbed, rolled in, and eaten when they show up.

Today, my brother, sister, and I travel paths that are very different from one another, but the connection we created from that experience remains with us.

IN 1989, EIGHT MONTHS AFTER Robert's death, I began my job as the lobbyist for the Washington State Nurses Association.

I've always been a somewhat private person, and at twenty-eight, having lived away from home for a while, I was not in the habit of talking about the people I was dating. But my sister, Lolly, knows me pretty well. One day when she called me to catch up, she asked me about my new job in Olympia. In between conversations about legislation she really wasn't interested in, the limited number of women lobbyists, which interested her even less, and whether I would be home for the weekend, she picked up on the serious excitement I was feeling in my new relationship with Art. In true family fashion, she hung up and called my parents.

"Something's up with Marianne," she told them.

The next morning, I got a call from my dad.

"I just happen to be driving down to Olympia today. Can I buy you lunch?"

We met for clam chowder by the bay, and he asked about my job, my new boss, and the other folks who worked in Olympia.

Finally, he said, "Your sister says you have a new friend."

Despite his faith in my decisions, he was convinced I had been hijacked by an old, fat, cigar-smoking, lecherous politician.

Over the next several months, my parents began to know Art, his story, and his background. They liked him. He was smart and engaging. He worked hard, a trait they admired. But my mom and dad had reservations about our potential future. They worried about the age difference and the timing. They worried about the fact that he had been married and was not divorced yet. They worried about blended-family dynamics. My dad, the youngest of six, had three half-siblings. His two half-sisters had had a complicated and acrimonious relationship with his mother, their stepmom. And my parents also knew how long "till death do us part" really meant, and about all the ups and downs that come in those years. They knew it was hard work. But they knew me, too. So despite their worries, when I told them Art and I had decided to marry, my dad, mom, and siblings had my back and walked in step with me.

Shortly after I met Katherine and Ashton on that New Year's weekend, I brought them to my folks' house to introduce them to my family. Over the summer months, we took them sailing on my dad's boat, the *Jubilee*, and had barbecues. We played dibble dabble in Lake Washington and played croquet on the front lawn.

After we married, my parents and siblings included my stepkids in family events and family trips. They paid for airfare and bought presents. It was not always a smooth voyage. In the same way I had to learn to navigate a relationship with this boy and this girl, my family had to also. We had lots of miscommunications. When my dad died, my brother asked me if I wanted to include them in the obituary as "survivors of." It caught me by sad surprise. Of course I did. They were his grandchildren, too.

It wasn't that my family did not accept my stepkids wholly, but a distance between them existed. It took some years for them to fully understand that I accepted Katherine and Ashton as "my own"—not just as my husband's kids. And in the same way that my stepkids did not choose a relationship with me, they certainly did not give much thought to my family's involvement in their lives.

Holidays were especially hard. My family traditions were not their family traditions. My mom served a Swedish smorgasbord every Christmas Eve, complete with raw herring and a bean dish called *bruna bönor*, and up to sixty family members attended this event. We wrote messages to Santa that we read aloud and sent up the chimney. I grew up with this, and I love it.

My new family was not so convinced. They had formerly spent their holidays with local, old family friends, including numerous kids who felt as close as cousins. They had ham. They missed those events when they were with us. And instead of spending the whole holiday at one house, there were late-night drop-offs and awkward goodbyes. Those first holiday years were very painful—you could have reached out and touched my stepkids' discomfort.

Incorporating everyone and their feelings into all the events over the years has continued to be difficult at times. My family knows and respects my stepkids' mother. They value her place in their life, and they inquire about her. In those first years, this may have created a bit of a divide for my family. Sometimes I wonder if this division would have existed if I had adopted children.

My family has been essential to my mental survival as a stepmom. They know me. They do not question my motivations or my commitment to Art or my stepkids. My parents and brother and sister were the primary observers of those tough first years, when my stepdaughter was furious and my stepson barely civil. They witnessed the pain of the town's relentless spite and offered assurances. They took my calls when subpoenas from Vicki arrived on birthdays. They asked no questions when I arrived at their house for lunch repeatedly—as in, on a daily basis—to watch *All My Children*. My sister invited us to gatherings with her friends, opening a door to a social life we so wanted for ourselves. They picked me up when I faltered and showed doubt, and reminded me of my capabilities. During the few times over the years when togetherness included old family friends or relatives on the Mother's side, my mom and sister and I invisibly linked arms and entered the not-always-welcoming den together.

Being a stepmom means not always knowing where you stand with people. I knew where I stood with my mom and dad and my brother and sister. And when my self-esteem and confidence began to wane, they were my glass of water in a lonely desert.

# 8

## OUR FAMILIES (HIS)

ART IS THE THIRD OF five children. He grew up in rural Pennsylvania. His dad drove a streetcar in Pittsburgh, and his mom taught at the local elementary school. His two brothers and two sisters rode horses, raised dogs, played sports, and worked on tomato farms. Athletic and smart, Art earned a basketball scholarship and went to college in New York. In time, all of his siblings went to college, left home, followed love and careers, and scattered across the States. Despite the many miles between them, they remain close.

In the two decades when Art and Vicki were together, they, along with their extended families, celebrated together, traveled together, laughed and argued together. They have many memories and picture books and a long shared history. They loved and enjoyed each other. Art's family is fond of Vicki. They were deeply saddened by the demise of their marriage, and I am sure they all missed her and felt a genuine loss.

"HI," I SAID TO HIS older sister on the phone in the winter of 1989.

It was my initial introduction to his family. I knew from my conversations with Art that they were somewhat wary of our relationship, worried about the same thing everyone jumped on: our age difference. But on this first phone call, I felt little, if any, suspicion. Wariness was replaced by curiosity. Conversation flowed easily. Our age difference was not apparent over the phone.

"I knew you must be someone special; he couldn't wait to get to the phone to call you every night," she laughed.

His older sister had just been visiting with Art in Florida, where the siblings had gathered to celebrate their parents' fiftieth wedding anniversary. We talked of the milestone celebration, her three kids, and her Arabian horses. We spoke of our hope of meeting each other soon.

Art's family's natural curiosity and loving protectiveness reached their peak that summer before we were married. They sent out a "spy"—my husband's thirteen-year-old niece— to assess the situation. We drove her to Mount Rainier to hike and marvel and walked through Pike Place Market, admiring the fresh-cut flowers and the fishmongers. She worried that we ate things with "eyes" (she was a new vegetarian), but by the end of her visit, she winked at me and concluded all was "okay." Three months later, her mom and his two brothers came out for our wedding and I met them in person for the first time. It was a hectic, short visit mixed with many wedding details.

During the first year of our marriage, my relationship with Art's family was mostly by phone. We had traveled to Florida to see his parents the morning after our wedding and attended a family reunion in North Carolina many months later, but finances, job realities, and distance did not allow us to see each other frequently.

I was aware that Vicki had stayed in contact with Art's family after their marriage was over. Cards, phone calls, and visits were all a part of those first years. I believe this continuing relationship was important to Ashton and Kate. Art's family also inquired about Vicki. When they saw the kids or talked to them on the phone, they asked how she was doing, how she liked her job. For me, these conversations were very appropriate. Vicki was their mother, a significant part of their life. Significant people and events should be acknowledged.

The first time Art's parents came west to Seattle after we had been married, they expressed their interest in seeing the mother of their grandchildren. With my blessing, they arranged to have lunch with Vicki one afternoon midway through the visit. Yes, it was sort of strange ("Bye-bye; see you soon"), but it was right and everyone survived. Plus, I got a new toaster out of it when they returned from lunch.

THREE YEARS INTO OUR MARRIAGE, it was our turn to host Art's family reunion. Twenty-five relatives—sisters, brothers, cousins, nieces, and nephews—were scheduled to fly in and, with luck, enjoy a multiday summer extravaganza with big meals, lousy sleep, stupid jokes, and lots of laughs. We were all looking forward to having this big group together. I planned menus, borrowed sleeping bags, and happily awaited their arrival.

One morning over a warm Dutch baby, while Art and I talked about the logistics of the upcoming gathering, Katherine asked if there would be time in the reunion for her mom to see everyone.

"I know she would really like to," she said to her dad, while watching me.

I smiled at her and did not say anything as I stood at the kitchen counter.

"You know, we really haven't worked out what we're going to be doing every day," replied her dad. "Why don't we see how it goes, and we can decide if it fits in later?"

"What do you think we should do?" I asked Art later that morning.

"I don't think we need to do it, but it's up to you," he said, looking at me. He would go along with my decision on this one.


THAT AFTERNOON, AS I MOWED the meadow, I thought about it. The family reunion was weeks away, and from that distance, a get-together with the first wife seemed doable. By now I had met everyone in Art's family and felt comfortable in my space with them. Despite our often-less-than-idyllic interactions with Vicki, making this blended family blend remained my hope.

*Don't let this be a big deal. Take control*, I said to myself. I could handle this event. It would be important for the kids.

So I marched up to the house, called Vicki on the phone, and invited her to dinner on an evening halfway through the family gathering. She agreed to come.

"My mom's excited to come for dinner," Kate said to me later that same afternoon after hanging up with her mom.

"That's good." I smiled at her. "I'm sure it will be nice for everyone to get together. The whole week should be fun, don't you think?"

I chose to focus on the entire reunion, not just that one night when Vicki was coming over.

THE DAY OF THAT DINNER started badly. Art, with all the enthusiasm of someone who thinks he can do everything, decided to take the reunion crew up to the vantage point of Washington Pass on the North Cascade Highway. It is a gorgeous and twisty round-trip drive of six hours, no stops included.

I leveled my eyes at him and said, "Please don't be late."

Off they went. I shook my head and knew deep down they would not be back in time. His sister, mom, and dad stayed behind to relax, read their books, and rest.

They were late.

The doorbell rang. I opened the door and heard a familiar "hi there." Even though Vicki was standing right in front of me, I felt thousands of miles away, watching her mouth move.

*Maybe this wasn't such a good idea*, I thought, as she walked through the front door and back to the living room. I watched as she entered and Art's three family members rose to greet her. Art's parents seemed uncomfortable. Actually, I thought we all looked a little awkward, as whether to hug or not to hug was pondered. But I suppose the first moments of anything can be that way. We all sat down in the living room, and Art's sister and parents caught up with her.

"How have you been?" "How is your job going?" "The kids look great! It's so good to see them."

I arranged the appetizers and sat in quiet observation. My jeans felt tight. I was hot. I fiddled with my hands. I went into the kitchen and lit the candle on the counter.

"Let's just finish making the dinner," I mumbled to myself. I flipped the marinating flank steaks and chopped up green onions for the rice dish. I found other things to do in the kitchen. I procrastinated while the conversation continued in the living room. I went back and forth from kitchen to living room, checking drinks and food. I rearranged the table settings. Finally, I heard the dogs bark. The group was back. This quiet house, thankfully, erupted into multiple voices and conversations.

It is still difficult to describe this evening. I often wonder what a stranger would have viewed if they had looked in on us. Would they have seen the play in full glory? Act three: dinner. Everyone loves the food; people are smiling, laughing, reminiscing.

Was it the reminiscing that bothered me? Was I really that insecure? But two-thirds of the way through the evening, I rose and quietly retreated. I walked upstairs to our bedroom. I looked out the window and listened to the conversation downstairs. I felt the familiar sting and quiver and quickly closed the bathroom door. Sobs escaped.

The upstairs of this house had a bathroom only a man would design. It was more like a hallway, a very convenient place in which to stop and pee as you walked through. And there I was, cold water running on my wrists, trying to pull myself together. It was one of those moments where you sort of see two of your selves, standing behind you in the mirror, one on each side. One says something like, *Pull it together, Lile,* and the other half says, *Shut up. Let it out.* I left the water on, hoping to stifle the noise of my tears. I was horrified, thinking that someone might come up and hear me.

I finally made my way back downstairs and poured myself a glass of red wine in the kitchen. I stood in there for a moment, breathing and looking out the window, and then joined the group back in the dining room. No one seemed to notice that I had been gone. They seemed to assume I had just left to use the bathroom. I was relieved. The evening was winding down. Dessert was being finished. The skies outside were growing dark. Vicki finally left. My new relatives scattered, some cleaning up in the kitchen, some heading to corners to read and relax, some going to watch a movie. My husband put on his favorite CD of the Moody Blues as a few of us sat on the deck outside.

My shoulders sank into my deck chair with defeat. Despite my hopes, I had let the evening get to me. I had let Vicki get to me. Her lack of acknowledgment, her smugness, her kids' happiness at her being there—I had let it all break me down. I was incredibly disappointed in myself.

I sat quietly in the chair on the front deck, listening half-heartedly to my brother-in-law and Art. Marlowe came outside, yellow night-night in tow, and climbed into my lap.

"Keep your eyes out for a shooting star," I said to her, holding her close. I hugged that beautiful girl, and while we both looked up at the night sky, I thought of a refrain from an old song we used to sing in high school: the Grateful Dead's "Truckin'."

As the song goes, the last few years had been strange. Good moments. Bad moments. In-between moments. But altogether not anything that I could have predicted or fully imagined.

Marlowe fell asleep in my lap. Art, my brother-in-law, and I stayed out there for some time, listening to the music and finishing our wine. I finally rose to take Marlowe upstairs and get ready for bed. I went to each visitor's bed and sleeping bag and placed a mint chocolate square on each pillow—a little treat that I had provided each night of the reunion. I finally crawled into my own bed. I went to sleep that night without talking about the breakdown in the bathroom with Art or with anyone. My disappointment in myself was for me alone. I would keep trying to do better the next time.

When I woke up the next morning, I did my best to shake off the bad juju of the evening. I laughed with my sister-in-law, talked books with my brother-in-law, and barbecued marinated leg of lamb with the relatives from California. We ate more chocolate mints and enjoyed the star-filled nights. We basked in the Northwest sunshine and the company of family. We looked forward to the next time we could all get together.

# 9

## LABELS AND DEFINITIONS

*OKAY,* I THOUGHT, *ANOTHER NEW year.* Another new set of fist pumps.

It was 1995, and I reached down into that imaginary, deep ocean in myself and pulled up a renewed surge of energy to go at this thing again.

Stepmom. I still found myself deliberating that expression often. It was the label that seemed to follow and define a big part of me and my life now. Who was that woman? What did she look like? What was she thinking? What did *stepmom* explain at this point about my marriage or my life?

The reality of my landscape is that it's quite hard to navigate around the word *mother.* It is a revered word. So, have we stepmoms—did I, as a stepmom—already set ourselves up for failure by competing with a goddess?

According to the dictionary, the definition of *mother* is

"someone who looks after, cares for, protects, nurses, or tends."

Even the definition of *adoption* has an affectionate nature: "acceptance, embracing, and taking on."

But the definition of *stepmother* is quite the opposite: "a woman who has married somebody's father after the death of or divorce from the person's mother."

Lucky me. I was simply that fortunate gal who got to marry the father. (And, truthfully, there were days when he did not exactly resemble the man who had taken me out for seafood.)

This definition from *Webster's* implied everything but what this stepmom—me—was actually doing. I have heard the phrase *gray area* all my life, but *stepmom* is the closest definition I have developed for that term.

*Gray area*: "unclear situation: a situation, subject, or category of something that is unclear or hard to define or classify."

From the get-go of this union in 1991, the word *stepmother* seemed to be loaded with tension. In a not-so-subtle way, it does conjure up a loss: death or divorce. Either way, it points to the demise of a relationship along the way.

And now I had this label attached to me.

What happens when you take on a label? If you become a doctor, you immediately have *MD* or *Dr.* attached to your name. It summons up a picture. Do pictures really tell a thousand words?

What words does the name *stepmother* summon? The most obvious one is *wicked*. It hangs there like a necklace. Even though I joked about that term with a sense of ridiculous irony, it was still out there, hovering, in close vicinity.

This wicked woman, complete with weird hair and suspicious eyes, was in our children's books and in the Disney movies. She was in magazines like *Vanity Fair*, in articles entitled "Wicked Stepmothers: They're Not Just in Fairy Tales." The stepmother with all her wickedness resides in our subconscious. Its implication is that a stepmom does not have your best interest in mind, is in some way conniving and malicious.

And I, this wicked stepmother, had the added fun of being labeled many other things, including a "homewrecker." There were folks in my community who believed I was the so-called immoral slut who wagged her tail at a man and led him down the path to adultery and betrayal.

And these folks were not very quiet about their thoughts. Ashton and Katherine had heard them. Often. Art and I had an uncomfortable discussion with them about it, explaining that the divisive comments about their dad and me were not true. We reminded them of when I had met their dad and the sequence of events. Art apologized again and again for the hurt he had caused them prior to meeting me. We explained the details as best we could.

But the community did not understand or care to listen. I did not shout the facts from the rooftop or write an op-ed for the local paper. I stayed quiet, waiting for the truth to rear its golden head. But as these first few years went by, it was hard to assure the only ones who mattered—Ashton and Katherine—that the words they had heard were just not the truth. And that was a hard space to live a life in.

Yep, at the end of his marriage, Art had had a short-lived affair with another woman. He had broken a vow. He had broken a trust. He had tremendously hurt three people he cared about. He deeply regretted it.

I am not bringing this up to be cavalier; I am not writing about this time period to gossip or share salacious stories. My man is a good man. He is not a thief. He is not a bum. He was not then, and is not now, a serial affair-taker. Yet that one poor decision appeared to be the only factor used to measure him from that moment on. Art and Vicki's friends took her side. And they took it hard. I never once witnessed or heard anyone say, "How hard this must be for *all* of you." No kind handshake was delivered, no understanding given. Art was alone. And he was vilified.

Why bring this up in a book about my experience as a stepmom?

Because I am not a trophy wife. I am not a member of some club, out to get older men's money. I am not a bimbo. I am not any of these hateful and misguided labels.

I am—and I think there are more like me than not—a gal who met a man, dated him, and got to know him. I was old enough to know what I was doing, and I was smart enough to have a good job and my own apartment. I was a gal who fell so deeply in love as to say, *I will take on everything about you—the divorce, the gossip, the dog, and the kids. Most important, the kids. We will be a family.* I accepted and embraced Ashton and Katherine as my own children and my own family.

Speaking to other stepmoms, I cannot imagine any other way to embrace this complicated scenario. You married a Dad with a capital *D*. More than likely, he loves his kids. He takes the role seriously. You live with him. You might be living with his kids. You do embrace them. You treat them with love. Despite all the strained conversations and the crying and sadness, you see them as vulnerable and exposed. You do your best to protect them. You may not have huffed and puffed for them in the delivery room, but you begin to feel them lingering in the recesses of your thoughts and in the marrow of your bones. You begin to love them and see them as absolutely necessary for the whole family photograph.

So—despite the tears and the tensions, despite the accusations and the anger, despite it all—I thought I had gotten through that first year and the second year in mostly one piece.

But labels and definitions are hard to shed. And though I was not really, fully aware of it, the tags being thrown out there into the cosmic dust of my world were sticking, and the balance of those labels was not matched by other ones. Just as the soccer field seemed to feel the weight of imbalance, the labels got pretty heavy. They stuck for years. They stuck to me.

There were times when my *stepmother* tag was one of my proudest labels. But over time, it gained weight and began to feel too sticky. There were always questions behind it. And as happens when you wear clothing that is too tight, there comes a time when you want to undo that button and just breathe free—no questions asked.

I wanted to throw that word—*stepmother*—into the shredder and just be the gal who was lucky enough to have met and married a man with two kids whom she grew to really love.

# I0

⁂

## THE EXERCISE CALLED PARENTING

$S$OMEWHERE ALONG THE WINDY, STRANGE path to adulthood, sayings and habits imprint themselves in your brain and come back to you as echoes. Some rise back from childhood ditties—*John and Mary, sitting in a tree, k-i-s-s-i-n-g,* or *Don't step on a crack, or you'll break your mother's back.*

I cannot recall where the following sayings emanated from or when I began to hear them rattling around, but there were three echoes that followed me ceaselessly in those first years of my marriage.

One: "What goes around comes around."

Two: "Just let a little time go by."

Three: "Never tell other people how to raise their children."

These adages trailed after me like tired and whiny little kids, bouncing around my brain, leaving moldy crumbs of doubt, worry, and irritation.

Number one: what goes around comes around. My friends often said this to me, pointing fingers at Vicki or the community in regard to their behavior toward me. But what I really wondered was, what had I done that was now coming around? What cosmic vibration had been altered? What curb had I tripped on, what misstep had I taken, that had propelled this ball of chaos around the corner to land at my feet?

This sentiment is usually balanced by the one that goes, "God doesn't give you things you can't handle." But while my religious beliefs and my cosmic beliefs were fighting it out above me, I was just trying to get out of bed and move forward.

Number two: time. While I understood that time was needed, what was that time going to actually reveal? The kind individuals who told me to "just let a little time go by" said it with the optimistic gusto that everything would be improved. But who out there in the world was guaranteeing that the inevitable days that passed were going to make things actually better and not worse? And, more importantly, what was I supposed to do while I waited for the time to go by? I must admit, I really disliked this one.

Which bring us to the third saying: never tell other people how to raise their children.

I do not know what voice whispered this notion into my consciousness. Did my mom used to say it? Did I pick it up in a magazine somewhere? Regardless, this adage is an intricate and tricky tap dance for any stepmom, and for me in particular.

I was living with these kids, at a minimum every other day and every other weekend. I was driving. I was alone with "Art and Vicki's" children a lot. I was not the nanny. I was not their friend. At the same time that I was asking them to take out the garbage or clean the rabbit cage, I was in a place where I had to make more significant decisions, important life decisions, from questions like "I'm going to Sammy's after school with Jimmy and Susie, okay?"—when I knew those kids were doing things they shouldn't be—to questions that could not wait for the standard reply, "Ask your dad when he gets home."

There were also instances when I found myself muttering, inwardly and silently, *I really don't enjoy that tone of voice you are using on me* or, *I'm thrilled that your boyfriend gets to do that over at your mother's house, but he isn't doing that over here.* This stepmom was in that place repeatedly. I had to make decisions at that moment, not later.

"MMM," I MUMBLED TO MYSELF one afternoon as I drove mindlessly over to Vicki's house to pick up Katherine. "They finally finished the construction on that house."

Around the curve, down the dip, up the hill, and a left turn. The sun was coming out behind the clouds. Marlowe slept quietly in her car seat in the back.

*I wonder whose car that is,* I thought as I pulled in behind it.

I noticed that the purple, white, and yellow irises were just beginning to bloom in Vicki's border garden next to the driveway as I walked up to the front door and knocked. I heard the sounds of feet scrambling behind the door, and I was turning to go back to the car, when it opened.

"Oh. Hi, Pete." I turned back around and spoke to Kate's boyfriend. "How are you?"

I looked at Katherine. "You ready to go, Kate? I'm kind of in a hurry, and I need to make a stop at the feed store before we head home," I said.

"Yep, just a sec; I need to grab my stuff," she replied, turning back into the house.

"How's soccer going?" I asked Pete.

"Oh, it's fine. It was nice not to have practice today." He smiled.

We looked around.

"Whose car is that?"

"It's my dad's."

"Did you drive it over?"

"Yeah," he grunted.

"Did you get your license?" I looked at him quizzically.

"Nope, not yet."

He looked at me and I looked at him.

I heard Kate jiggling the keys as she locked the front door.

I looked at the ground and over at the irises.

"Well," I said slowly, "how are you going to get home?"

No reply.

"Can one of your parents come over to get you? Or were you going to walk?"

Kate marched down the stairs to the driveway to stand between us.

"Mar," she interrupted, "it's fine. He can drive home. He's driven over here before."

I shrugged my shoulders.

"Well, it's really not okay with me."

"Mar!" Rolling her eyes, she looked at Pete.

"I can't let him drive home, knowing he doesn't have his

license. I'm sorry. What if someone hit him or if he hit something? It'd be a mess." I looked at them both.

"Don't make such a big deal about it. He's just driving home. It's fine," Katherine repeated, with growing annoyance.

"No," I sighed, "it's not."

I opened the car door. I looked at Marlowe.

"Is your mom or dad around to come get you?" I asked Pete.

"They're probably still at work," he said. Katherine's simmering agitation was obvious. I recognized all the signs.

"Okay, c'mon," I said to them. "Get in." I figured he would just take the car after I left. "I'll have to take you home."

"I can't believe you're making such a big deal about this!" Kate hissed at me. "God, just let him drive it home! This is so stupid!"

I looked at her and got in my car. Marlowe had woken up, and I smiled at her as I waited for them to grab Pete's stuff from the cab of the truck and get in my car.

I watched as they both got out and whispered to each other, and then Pete turned around to walk to his front door. Kate got back in the car and slammed the door. We did not talk. Those silences end up saying so much.

It was the millionth or trillionth disagreement we had had over the years. As we drove to the feed store, the familiar weariness sank in.

IN THE BIG QUILT OF family life—the interweaving threads, the blended colors, the jagged edge, the cushy middle—these "events" are all catalysts that slowly reveal who you are, and your opinions and values become part of the framework of family life. Your beliefs get out there without even noticing. But my family quilt was just getting started and, only a few years in, my opinions, beliefs, and values were not common knowledge to my stepkids yet.

But our situation often required me to make the call, to express my thoughts and, right or wrong, say yes or no.

I went by my gut. But just as my decision-making priorities were not common information to my stepkids, my gut was not in top parental shape, either. It had not been there for the years of buildup that parents experience while, slowly but constantly, it morphs into an instinctual patience that teaches parents when to let something go, when to keep quiet, or when to express their thoughts.

I was brand-new to parenting. My entrance collided with a parenting model that was over a decade in the making. Art and Vicki had been, and continued to be, good parents together. While they did not always agree, they had behind them years of making decisions and choices regarding the upbringing of their kids. That partnership did not go away with the divorce. Art and, to a lesser degree, Vicki had the challenge of now dealing me in.

My stepkids were stuck, too. They had not been in a position to interview the new person in their life who would be making decisions, and I had not been in a role of "authority" when Art and I dated. But, wham! Thrust upon them soon after we signed the legal document of marriage, this woman, this stepmom, was now standing before them and trying to resolve important issues for them. Choices had to be made, and my fallback stance of "ask your dad" was always not realistic or convenient.

There were a lot of mistakes on my part. More than once, I overreacted and expected certain behaviors that I would have expected in "my" children.

There was the afternoon when Ashton had borrowed Art's car. I got his phone call midday.

"Mar, I was in an accident."

"Are you okay? Where are you?"

I packed up Marlowe and drove down into town, where he stood next to the Honda. The back window was completely smashed and gone. Glass was everywhere.

Ash stood quietly when he saw me coming.

"Are you sure you're okay?" I asked him again.

He was fine. He really did not appear to be worried about anything: the broken window; the fact that it was going to rain later. He seemed, in fact, indifferent by the fact the car had been in an accident at all.

I got mad.

The new business was not bringing in much money. Art and I were both stressed about our income, our business expenses, and staying ahead of the bills. I had spent that entire morning trying to reconcile the income and debts we were assuming. And that broken back window was not going to be cheap. We had a high deductible on our car insurance.

"You need to go get the window fixed," I said to him bluntly. "It's going to rain, and your dad has to use the car this week for work. We'll put it on the insurance, but you'll have to pay the deductible."

He looked at me blankly. "I don't have the money."

"Well, you'll have to take it out of your savings, I guess."

We looked at each other, staring, like in a Western standoff.

"I want it fixed before your dad gets home."

"Mar." He looked at me with surprise.

I turned and walked back to my car.

I knew I was overreacting. I knew I should back off. He was just a kid who had messed up. Instead of taking a deep breath and counting to ten, I let the issues of the rest of the day overwhelm me, and I took it out on him. I had not yet developed my instinctual parental patience.

Ashton complained later to his dad about my reaction. I'm sure he complained to his mom, too. I knew that Art and Vicki would have handled it differently. I wished I had, too.

AS MUCH I ADMIRED KATHERINE'S willingness to debate an issue, her language was appalling. She threw the *f*-word at her mom, and she threw it at her dad.

"I would never have been able to talk to my parents like that," I said to Art in frustration and disbelief. "I cannot believe that you and Vicki let her get away with it."

"I don't always let her get away with it. You need to look at the whole picture, Mar. I don't like it either, but we need to pick and choose our battles with her."

When Ashton fell in love for the first time, it was a real awakening to me. His obliviousness to anything around him besides this girl bugged the whole family. I thought there should be limits on how late and how often he was seeing this gal.

Art's response stopped me in my tracks and reminded me, again, of my parental learning curve: "How many times in your life do you actually fall in love? Let's let them enjoy it—within reason. It happens too infrequently to squash it down."

I had a lot to learn. I had to hurry and catch up to where the mom and dad were in this parental equation. Not only did I have to catch up, I had to try to align my opinions with the ones they had held for many years already. I did not always agree with their opinions, and we were not always on the same page about all the issues before us.

We had a lot of issues before us.

As is often the case, money was a monumental issue.

Money. Money. Money. There is never enough of it, even if there is.

I have not met one couple—blended or non-blended—who at some point have not had a disagreement, argument, or major dispute over family finances.

I believe blended families come with their own distinct set of financial pressure points. It sits there on the table at the first of the month when you pay the bills, which oftentimes include child support or alimony. It sits there in the middle of the month, when some unexpected expense arises and no one can agree on whose household will pay for it. It is a constantly simmering pot of water, ready to burn someone.

In my case, there were three people—Art, Vicki, and I— trying to establish our own financial objectives and dreams. At the same time, our budgets overlapped with each other's, as both parents were intricately involved with the day-to-day and future expenses that surrounded the kids. Art and I had certain ideas of where and how we wanted to meet our goals, and I'm sure Vicki did, too. Predictably, the dreams of these two households were not on the same page. Often, they were in separate chapters of separate books. Thus, the conflicts swirled. Sometimes they were small, sometimes they were huge, but they were there on the kitchen table every single month.

The first two married people, Art and Vicki, had been making financial decisions together for a long, long time. They knew how the other person felt about finances and how their minds worked to resolve different financial issues. They knew what buttons to push to get a desired result or to nag. Their money was in one pot.

Now that I was in the financial picture, I brought my own ideas into this triangle. For years prior to my marriage, I had paid my own way and had my own stubborn ideas about finances—as a single person.

I was prepared to share financially with Art, and I understood and supported his child support and alimony obligations before we got married. But merging financially with another person is complicated, and when I moved in, the mortgage was already in place, college for my stepkids was not very far off, and the fees for pricey activities, such as select sports, had been agreed upon.

Plus, all the money was now in several pots. There were different bank accounts, separated retirement accounts, and new, divorced financial worries.

A divorce agreement might outline every minute detail of who is buying what (theirs did not), but I think there will still be disagreements. Change happens. Priorities shift. The roof needs to be replaced at the same time the furnace decides it has had enough of this life. People lose their jobs, and incomes change. A third person has a different point of view. It is the highest of tight-wire acts to navigate.

Tough, tense, and disagreeable—three words I have heard other stepparents use when discussing trying to figure out money issues in a blended family. These words certainly describe the budgetary circumstances of my married life. And that was just between Art and me. Adding in Vicki and her priorities created an extremely complicated relationship for us. It strained our every ability to be rational and reasonable. Art and I quickly learned which buttons we could push in each other, both positive and negative. And our personality differences shone through when we discussed our family budget. Art is logical and scientific, more of a line-item kind of guy. I am more creative and not that scientific. My philosophy could be summed up as "this much money for one pot, and this much money for another pot."

"What exactly did you buy at Costco?" he'd ask.

"Stuff for the house, dog food, the usual," I'd reply.

"What is 'the usual'?"

"You know, stuff we ran out of, stuff we need."

Going into detail about how many rolls of toilet paper we used each month or how much dishwasher soap cost was never going to be the way I spent my time.

Some months this difference in our personalities would escalate. As the primary purchaser of monthly items, I rarely went over budget, but it fell to me to explain every purchase.

"Don't you trust me to stay within our limits?" I'd ask.

"Sure ... *but* how much does the milk we drink each month cost?"

"You need to trust me ... or go and do it yourself one month."

I ACCEPTED THE EXPENSES THAT were already in place, and I worked hard to be balanced in my opinions. But inevitably, my irritation would build as decisions I was not a part of would dictate how "my" household money got spent, on both small things (does she really need the most expensive soccer shoe on the market?) and big things (can he at least consider the full scholarship to that college?). Even the simplest of decisions, like refinancing, quickly became less than simple because of the divorce agreement.

Rational and irrational emotional responses often collided. Irrationally, if Art had failed to mention some expense—even if I might agree with the decision—my crazy, pissed-off side could rise out of the ashes, my hair smokin' in all directions.

Rational disagreement occurred, too, once my hair was finally smoothed down. But in a triangle, you can be outvoted.

Meanwhile, Art's job loss and the realities of our new medical practice multiplied and magnified the financial burden. We continued to invest conservatively in the business, purchasing materials and hiring staff at the bare minimum of what was required. Our patient caseload was nowhere near the level it had been previously. Art spent many hours soliciting referrals and networking with other physicians, but the growth of the business and, consequently, of our income was slow.

The truth is that, in a very real sense, you are not always talking only about money. You are also tackling the highly charged emotions and different egos that are hidden in those discussions—the passions behind why this couple got divorced in the first place, the frustration behind why they did not figure this out better beforehand, the loathing that you even have to deal with it at all.

In my stepmom group and during the subsequent years, I met stepmoms who complained a lot about their struggles with money. Some had a lot of cash in the bank; some had just a little. But the sentiment was very similar to my own experience: the stepmom is usually at the bottom of the decision-making process regarding how money is spent for the kids and consequently for the whole family.

I met one stepmom who told me her husband's ex-wife was getting their kids' college tax credit, even though she was not spending any of her money on the children's college. This former couple had agreed that she would receive the tax credit and that she would then reimburse the dad for the sum, but later she called and said, "Why should I?" I heard about, witnessed, and experienced many other, similar tales.

WHEN ART LOST HIS JOB, we continued our full payment of child support based on his previous income. To adjust the amount of support would have required lawyers and meetings and time, and we were not remotely interested in taking Vicki back to court over that issue and thereby adding even more financial and emotional headaches to our day-to-day existence. Plus, deep down, I believe Art and I thought this was a momentary "bump"—not a situation that in fact it would take us years to recover from. So we wrote the checks. We paid for our full portion of college, we wrote the check for select soccer, and we wrote the check for all the incidentals. We paid without regret. But it was hard. And I believe that my stepkids got very confused and mad about all the bickering and haggling. (*I* got mad about all the bickering and haggling!) But kids do not know the ins and outs of what working ten hours a day actually means. Ashton and Katherine did not know that the select soccer team that cost $1,000 was a huge chunk of our monthly income, now that their dad had lost his job and we were starting a new business. And we did not want them to know the minute details of every expense and worry more about anything than they already were.

Art and I sat down with the kids and explained the new realities as best we could. We talked with them frequently and honestly. They always sat down when asked. They appeared attentive. But they did not reciprocate with a lot of feedback or commentary. They had "teenage head." Unless an issue affected them directly, I think it was difficult for them to fully comprehend. And they still had that natural "out" of going to their mom's every other day, so our money issues were not constantly in their field of vision.

We were also battling with our instinctive protectiveness towards them. You do not really want things to change any more drastically than they already have for these kids. You want them to have things they had before, and better things, too. After all, they are children of divorce. This was one of the unspoken philosophies. They were scarred. They had been hurt. And we sometimes overcompensated by agreeing to and paying for activities and toys, then calling the other parent on the phone and arguing about who was going to cover the cost.

Money was at the forefront of our minds most every day

for that first year after Art lost his job and we started our own business. We went to bed thinking about it and woke up in the middle of the night thinking about it. Once in a while, we would look at each other and say, "We can't live like this. Things are going to improve. We need to do something fun to break out of this cycle"—normal, fun activities like a camping trip to Mount St. Helens. But even normal, fun things could get complicated and pivot in directions we never could have foreseen.

Our camping trip to Mount St. Helens was planned. We had four days and three nights ahead of us as a family. We were all going to go car camping with tents and sleeping bags and s'mores. In a few weeks, at the end of the summer, Ashton was going to be leaving again for college. He had had a good first year. Despite having not made the soccer team, he had excelled—thrived—in his new environment. Still the achiever, he had joined groups, played intramurals, participated in student government, and succeeded academically. He had made a lot of new friends. He loved California and all the activities the climate allowed. In his spare time, he hiked and rock-climbed and headed to the beach. His college hair was now a little longer and a little lighter.

His first summer at home had sped by, and we had not had any time to get away and try to relax, all five of us. Away from the medical practice that was sputtering to survive. Away from the lawyers we were seeing weekly in the lawsuit we had filed against Art's former employer.

A simple, normal family vacation.

Mount St. Helens had erupted fifteen years earlier, and none of us had been down to see the mountain in years. As we drove along the Spirit Lake Memorial Highway, the devastation from the volcano remained dramatic. On one side, the terrain looked as if Mother Nature had carried on quietly and unobtrusively. Green plants grew up around the trees. Wildflowers that had bloomed earlier now scattered on the wind. If we turned our heads to the other side of the road, we were in a different landscape, a different country. Mother Nature had shown her full force of violence with a combustible combination of fire, ash, and heat. Total devastation. Even fifteen years later, we could view the full impact and imagine the immensity of the eruption. Black and gray covered the terrain. Burned and dead tree trunks littered the area but somehow remained standing, despite the strong winds, rain, and snow that pelted them every year. Remnants of scorched cars remained, parked, on the side of the road.

We toured the east side and peered down at Spirit Lake, now blocked by thousands of drowned logs. We all sat and pondered the immensity of this change in the lake and the surrounding area. At the end of the day, we finally found our campsite.

"How do you guys like this one?" Art asked our passengers.

"Whatever, Dad—just pick one. We need to get out the car," Kate replied quickly.

We pulled out the tents and poles and stared at the directions and, with a little personality push and pull between father and children—"I know how to do it"; "No, I *know* how to do it!"—got those two tents up. One tent for us and Marlowe, and one tent for Ashton and Katherine. We unpacked the coolers and found some wood for the campfire. It had been a long day in the car. We were all hot and sticky.

"Is it okay if we go exploring for a little while?" they asked their dad.

"Sure. Just be back in thirty minutes."

Ash and Kate looked a little suspicious about their desire to go "explore," but Art and I looked at each other and, in our growing parental partnership, let this one go.

I pulled out the food and started chopping onions. I had found an article on car-camping meals in *Gourmet* magazine the week before and had done the majority of the prep work before we left home. Four steaks had been marinating for the last twenty-four hours in Ziploc bags in a scented mixture of balsamic vinegar, olive oil, rosemary, garlic, and roasted red peppers. The rice would be mixed with the onions and the parsley. I husked the corn while enjoying a glass of red wine. Art sat down to help with the corn, and we watched Marlowe thumb through her favorite books by the tent. I knew the kids were tired and cranky, and I hoped this meal would partly solve the problem. It was meant to be a special treat on our first night of camping.

Kate and Ash got back to the campsite, and the five of us ate in a circle, talking about the day we were ending and the parts of the mountain we were going to see in the subsequent days.

The corn was buttery, the rice was fluffy, and while I know that all food tastes great when you are camping, I thought the steaks tasted pretty darn good, too.

Over the next three days, we toured the other sides of the Mount St. Helens national park. We hiked up the trails and visited the learning center, peering at the before and after pictures and reading the firsthand accounts of the eruption in 1980.

We had some laughs mixed in with some forced family togetherness. Marlowe was a toddler, and she acted that way. She smiled and laughed; she cried and threw tantrums. Mostly, she babbled through each day. She told stories to herself and anyone who would listen, looking up to her two older siblings for some reaction. They smiled and laughed a lot, and sometimes they did not want to be bothered. But we rallied and played cards and joked by the campfire. By the fourth day, we had seen all sides of the mountain and we were ready for the drive home.

It was quiet in the car, and we were almost back to the house. I cannot remember how it started, but once it began, it was like the erupting mountain we had just left. Heat and lava gushed out of my stepson's mouth. He yelled in frustration and anger.

"You're just so damn stingy and cheap, Dad! Kate and I aren't allowed to do anything. You're constantly yelling at us about money! You go on and on about how much that thing costs and how we're going to pay for it. You can be such a jerk! And then look at what Marianne does. She buys steak for dinner! And you let her!" he shouted at his dad. "I don't want to hear about it anymore!"

It was an argument of harsh words and a lot of pent-up fury. My normally reserved stepson had found his voice, and he let us have its full effect. He let his dad know what seemed like every supposed slight he had ever felt.

I looked at Art as I gathered Marlowe and left the car to take her away, up to the house. His face was such a sad mixture: flustered, frustrated, but mostly just full of real, deep hurt.

"I'll wait for you up at the house," I said.

He nodded.

I waited, pacing from room to room. I was so surprised by this outburst. It was unexpected. I was angry at the kids for blaming Art and not showing any understanding toward him or me. I was also a little resigned and sad for Ashton and Katherine.

An hour later, the three returned with red eyes and flushed cheeks. The kids got their stuff and left quietly for their mom's house.

It was a huge fight over steaks, but really it was an emotional release of all the passions that circled overhead, underneath, and in between us. Eventually, these passions overwhelmed one of us and we erupted—about money, rules, and all the different and varied events that had happened over the last few years. Each of us had left what was familiar and had been thrown into the space of the unknown, and at times it was simply too much to handle. This argument over steaks was two steps back after three steps forward.

OF ALL OUR MANY ISSUES, money and our different views on it remained a big hindrance in our efforts to blend. Our two households never really figured out a good way to deal with our combined financial issues. We had many more quite heated conversations about money with both Vicki and the kids in the years ahead. We tried to tackle each one as they came up, and did so sometimes successfully, sometimes not. As with a lot of our blended-family struggles, I looked ahead to a time when we could take the combined pot off the stove and throw it out the window.

꧁꧂

# BEHIND CLOSED DOORS

*M*Y STEPSON WENT BACK TO college, my stepdaughter entered her senior year of high school, and my daughter went from toddler chatter to full-on sentences and stories. There was laughter. There was good food. We danced to Ella and Louis with Marlowe and went to more soccer games with Katherine. We sang the entire soundtrack to *Jesus Christ Superstar* with friends from Seattle on New Year's Eve and listened to our pet doves coo in the solarium.

The initial folks whom I had met in town still left me hanging, but once in a while an interaction would occur that surprised me to my core. There were approximately ten families with homes on the hill when I moved into Art's house. Surrounded by trees and space, we saw each other sporadically, waving from the car window or bumping into each other at the row of mailboxes that sat at the bottom of the hill. The layout of the houses created a vast amount of privacy, but the neighbors I met were friendly and open. Our interactions circled around the road issues we were all responsible for and the care of our pets when we left on vacations.

Sandy and her husband had lived on the hill for many years when I met her, raising their kids and enjoying our small-town community and rural life. She laughed every time I called to have one of her kids feed our growing animal family; I always seemed to have added a new pet to the roster. One afternoon, she drove up to the house when her daughter was unable to make it and had me show her the latest animal lineup before we left for a long weekend. We spoke randomly of the weather and our well-water issues, and then I walked her to the door to leave.

"Thanks so much for coming up. I really appreciate you all taking such good care of the pets."

"It wasn't a problem. You guys have a nice weekend."

As she turned to walk down the steps to her car, she paused and looked back at me.

"I just want you to know, Art seems really happy."

I was so surprised, I almost reached out and hugged her close. "Wow," I said to her. "Thank you for saying that."

I remain incredibly grateful for this interaction.

Art and I were happy-ish, but the weight of those early years, striving to figure out the definition of and being a "wife," confronting step-parenting, becoming pregnant and having a baby, attempting to have some sort of a relationship with the Mother, and my lack of acknowledgment from members of my community had all taken a toll on me.

Physically, I was more than tired. I was more emotional.

I cried often. I was "off." My sense of myself felt diminished. It seemed like my "self," whatever that was made up of, was fluttering back and forth, trying to right itself. I became disheartened and depressed. Without being aware of it, every time I sat and paused, I left a part of me—a slice of personality or a bit of confidence—on the ground when I stood up again. But I didn't feel lighter.

Disheartened. Depressed. Diminished. It's not as if you are even aware that these big adjectives are sneaking up on you. I certainly was not. They just started taking residence inside me, sneaking into my dark interiors, finding a place to lie, and padlocking themselves in for the ride.

I got paranoid and mistrustful. I lost my oomph—my get-up-and-go. I started grocery shopping in the next town. I was not always excited to go to Katherine's or Ashton's events. I began to recognize cars and to avoid them. I quit trying to make conversation and waited for it to come to me. I retreated. I had lost part of me, myself, and I.

I still functioned—lived—oftentimes even fully and happily. But there was a lingering dark shadow right there with me, a backpack full of heavy items—the disheartened item, the depressed item, and the diminished item—ready to take over, sometimes for an hour, sometimes for a day, sometimes for a week.

I still laughed and made jokes. I cooked great food. I changed my hairstyle and color literally every six months. I had the best hairstylist on the planet, and Gary experimented with everything—from bangs, to multicolored layers, to Annie Lennox–short peroxide blond (he called it Little Kitty), to the darkest black. I changed it so often, Marlowe's swim teacher asked if I was in a theater group. I had fun with my hair, and it kept my stepkids and husband on their toes. On the one hand, it was also the only thing I had left of my old life of freedom and individuality, but it may have also been an attempt to morph into someone else and see if I fit in.

I honestly can't say that I ever really did. With many of the new people I met, I was either overly cautious and quiet or overly friendly and loud. I wondered what they had heard, what they thought. I often tried way too hard. I sabotaged many potential friendships. I found myself increasingly isolated.

One of the worst things about isolation is that it makes you doubt—doubt your life and your decisions. It made me question this great love that I had found because we did not meet the expectations of what love should look like. Doubt can take you back to your worst insecurities and your worst thoughts about yourself. It did this to me.

I carried this heavy backpack filled with all these doubts and adjectives for a long while. Over time, I turned around and tried to go back and look for the parts I had left behind, but I'm afraid that some are lost forever. Today, I find myself still a little isolated. It has become a bit of my nature.

Art changed, too. He was like a tree trunk in the woods, with some pretty nasty scars from storms past. He hardened up some. The weight of being fired and the subsequent lawsuit against his former employer was intense. We were both forced to stay so positive, so sure, that that was its own type of exhaustion. The lawsuit forced us to rehash things over and over, and his firing forced us to face real economic hardship. It was hard to be honest with each other about our real fears and anxieties. One slip, one sidestep of doubt, had the tendency to stay in our thoughts, so it was best to try to be upbeat, or we might never recover. My emotional and physical shifts—my diminished, depressed, and disheartened self—had an effect on him, too. He worried. He stressed. Once in a while, he erupted in frustrated anger.

The obvious consequence of all this was a weakened marriage. Our union had altered. Amid all these different and jarring changes, how could it not have? We had lost a lot of elements along the way. It had become something neither one of us recognized or desired. We had stopped taking true care of each other. We were not companions but roommates. While our relationship still looked forward, we walked separately, the majority of our thoughts and concerns kept within. We passed each other without taking the full measure of where we were. We were cautious, not wanting to argue or disagree. We had lost our ability to laugh at ourselves and break the bad karma circling above us. Our relationship had lost its essentialness. Once again, we chose to go back to marriage counseling and, again, hoped it would give us some assistance or solutions.

I have a love-hate relationship with marriage counseling. The premise is sound, and I believe that it is helpful to talk with an expert in the field and attempt to get out of the rut in which your marriage is spinning its wheels.

But first you have to find a good expert. That is extremely hard. Do you get a man or a woman? Do you choose a certain philosophy, such as a John Gottman expert, or choose a practitioner who has cherry-picked wisdom over the years and formed their own opinion of what works?

There are limited reviews for marriage counselors, so you tend to pick one somewhat blindly.

It takes several visits to figure out if the one you picked is going to meld with your two personalities. These are expensive visits to try something out. Yes, it is cheaper than divorce, but when insurance doesn't cover this expense, and you are already at your limit on monthly expenditures … well, adding a weekly $120–200 per hour to that balance sheet put both Art and me on edge even before we had gotten into the car to drive to the counselor's office. We debated with each other about the necessity of this step. We were smart, weren't we? Couldn't we really figure this out ourselves, maybe go to a hotel for a couple of weekends instead? But this debate between us was just talk, not action. Picking up the phone, making the actual appointment, and agreeing to pay someone is the incentive to make you actually show up.

We got through the get-to-know-you visits, usually three, and then came the visit where each person goes alone to talk with the counselor. You are asked not to talk to your spouse about what the counselor said to you during that visit. I found that restriction somewhat ridiculous. One big fight, and the other person would be quick to say, "The counselor says you are [insert some personality flaw]. So there—I've been right all along!" Then you return, week after week, discussing one particular issue that occurred the week before. Fifty minutes is over before you know it. Sometimes we left with a lighter load. Sometimes we left angry. Sometimes we left upset. But we showed up.

Art and I ended up being short-term marriage counseling clients. At the time, it was hard to schedule an hour away from our new business practice and make sure child care was covered, and the expense of these weekly visits got to both of us. We had so many issues before us that one hour per week was going to necessitate a long, long time to get through each one and find a safer way to navigate. Usually, within three to six months, we would finally look at each other and say, "We need to do this on our own. We need to make our own appointments with each other."

However, even the short-term visits helped. We may have stopped short of tackling some of the biggest issues with the professional on the couch, but we did enough damage control to move forward with more optimism. We were able to shift the focus back to us. And sometimes that's all you need to be willing to do in a marriage.

All marriages are work. Blended marriages are a real labor of love. Art and I had never been together, married, without children. And they did not start out as babies or even toddlers in our marriage. They had voices and opinions and emotions. We added another baby to the mix and experienced all the same stresses that non-blended families have when they have a new baby—no sleep, no sex, no real time for each other. Add in all the rest—loss of income, grief, depression, anxiety—and the fact that all this had happened before we had been married five years, and our marriage looked at times like a blown-up balloon ready to burst.

But for whatever reason, we hung in there, even though we talked about leaving. Leaving just did not seem right. It did not make sense to us to create one more household, one more limited bank account, one more hurt child.

That is not to say it was easy. We gave up a lot. We both

saw each other in unfavorable ways. We had to be willing to sacrifice some of the things that we saw in each other when we dated. We had to be willing to understand that the life-blow the other person was experiencing might change them a little, and that we would have to get to know that new trait. We had to try to forgive each other, and when we couldn't do that, we had to at least walk away from thinking about it so much.

Road trips have always been good for Art and me. So we took road trips. We locked each other in the car, listened to our music, and drove wherever the whims of the day took us. We camped, saw gorgeous country, and renewed the embers of the love that, according to the cards, had been going on through many, many past lives. So far, so good.

## 12

⚜

# THE MOTHER

"OKAY, MOM. UH-HUH. OH, THAT sounds like fun. How funny. Yep. Okay. Talk with you later. Love you, too. Bye."

Katherine hung up the phone and sliced some cheese from the plate on the counter.

"How's your mom?" I asked her happily.

We had had a good afternoon. Katherine had gotten a haircut, and we had gone shopping. A girls' day. It was a rare evening when this senior in high school stayed home with us for the night. She was working on her college applications and looking forward to the end of high school and the start of something brand-new.

I stood in the kitchen, chopping up onions and red and yellow peppers for the pizza we were making. Art would be home soon. Earlier, we had picked up several good movies from the video store, and we were ready to press PLAY when he arrived.

"Oh, she's good. She's having a little party tonight at her house."

"That sounds like fun."

"Her girlfriends are all getting together for wine and cheese, and then they're going to see that movie *The First Wives Club.*"

She looked at me quickly as she laughed.

"Oh." I laughed with her. "How funny."

I smiled at her as we talked about the difficult choice of whether to put Italian sausage, pepperoni, or both on the pizza.

To my inner self, I said *fuck* and rolled my eyes. I had mastered the art of having two conversations at the same time—one out loud and one internally.

*Are you kidding me?* I said to myself.

This was so typical. Vicki. Her friends. *The First Wives Club.* Spiteful women getting back at their loser husbands.

I continued my internal conversation. *Why the hell would she tell Katherine this?*

I turned on the oven and walked into the family room. I opened up the glass door to the fireplace, grabbed some logs, and threw them on the fire.

*Why do these sentiments have to be continually rehashed?* I wondered.

Here we were, five years later, and Vicki was still carrying on with the same themes. With her girlfriends, with her daughter, with the community. Vicki and her group were in the "first" club. The right club. The rules and actions of this club were somehow justified by the numerical order in which the members had arrived on the scene. The other side of this thought process was that there was a wrong club. A less-than-honorable group. These themes continued to be revisited constantly. Overtly and inadvertently. On birthdays, at holidays, and still at the inevitable soccer games.

I could not even tell whether at this point Vicki and her friends were doing all this on purpose or if it had simply become muscle memory and reflex for them. But I was tired and pissed off that their behavior continually resurfaced. Equal footing, equal lives—would it ever just be?

At that point, I would have liked to imagine that these thematic rhythms would have disappeared. That after all these years, and given the in-your-face reality that I was still married to Art, had a new child with him, and was still residing in this house on the hill and in the community, all would have become wine and roses, songs being sung in the streets in happy harmony.

But we were not there yet.

Perhaps these themes were never supposed to go away. Maybe it was simply unrealistic of me to believe that an assimilation of good feelings and good spirits would ever arise. The themes changed some, morphed into tangents, but they remained.


ASHTON AND KATHERINE QUITE CLEARLY had a mother. A good mother. And they worried about their mother—a lot. I believe that most kids in blended families carry a special pocket of concern and anxiety for their moms.

In my effort to care for Kate and Ash and to demonstrate to them the priority that they were in my life, I privately thought a lot about Vicki, too. Consequently, many of my decisions regarding Vicki started from the premise of what I could do to make my stepkids feel better, to move forward with as little worry from them as possible. I thought about her feelings. I tried to predict how she might react to some situation, and then I did whatever I could to make that same situation as conflict-avoidant as possible. It was easy to sit in the back if Vicki sat up front. If we arrived at the same time, we would let Vicki walk through the door for the first entrance, and then we would follow.

It also meant responding to the worries that the kids might communicate or demonstrate. When my dad got sick and Katherine saw all the care that he received from my family, she expressed her worry about her parents' future care needs.

"Don't worry," I joked with her. "If worse comes to worst, I'll put them side by side upstairs and take care of them with you. We'll have our own little family-care station."

I would pretend that it did not bother me every time Kate or Ash brought up some sack of stuff, usually really old stuff, that Vicki had been cleaning out and thought Art might like to have all these years later.

It often meant including their mom when activities or events fell on "our" weekend or night. The activities ranged from birthdays to holidays to graduations. They also included less specific occasions. It was not always fun, and it was not always easy. I got especially annoyed when Vicki came up to the house and, seemingly every visit, commented on the rock with the fossil imprint that was placed on the corner of the stone wall surrounding the Russian fireplace.

"Did you know that Art and I found that together up in the mountains?"

Well, yes, I did.

I also met with Vicki privately on many occasions during those first years. I had quickly tossed aside the unspoken rule regarding conversations with the Mother and thought direct conversation might be more beneficial, but these meetings were not always very helpful. In those first five years, there was not a lot of generosity from her. But, to everyone's credit, we tried.

Gathering together in public and even in private required a different sort of energy. It was a mix of love and tenderness for the kids and a requirement of our family responsibilities. We had to gear up for it, as if downshifting on a steep hill. Sometimes we were reluctant. Occasionally we were in a bad mood and simply unwilling to try. Now and then, some event we were looking forward to would take a turn in a direction we were not expecting and we would leave shaking our heads at this bizarre situation.

Public events where we all assembled were often the most difficult. Simple greetings or acknowledgment of each other upon arrival could be met in two ways—friendly, with a wave, or invisible, with a turn of the shoulder.

There were also instances in which folks who would not give me the time of day in front of Vicki discovered their hypocritical side when she was not present. One day, I sat down on the hard bleachers at school in the spring sunshine, waiting for the track meet to begin. I looked around at the empty seats, enjoying a moment of quiet with the sun on my face. I heard the steps behind me and turned around.

"Oh, hi, Jim." I said, surprised.

"Hi. How are you? Nice day for a track meet."

It was a pleasant fifteen-minute conversation. But this gentleman, married to one of Vicki's closer friends, had never before had a real conversation with me in the five years that I had seen him at all of the events in which we were joint participants.

In a strange coincidence, Vicki dated a man Art and I had known from Olympia. He and I had even gone out for a drink once. I saw him from across the bleachers at a game one evening. As I approached him to say hello, I recognized the sign of apprehension and reluctance to converse. It was almost as if a rulebook had been given out to people in the "club."

Every once in a while, we gathered and it did click. We would all genuinely laugh, find some semblance of solidarity, and in fellowship leave the event without the sting of awkwardness and dissatisfaction. It gave me a sliver of hope for the next occasion.

To celebrate Kate's high school graduation, the members of her family gathered on the front deck at the house on the hill in genuine happiness. My mom was there. Ashton was home. Marlowe twirled in her dress, excited to have her brother and sister together again. Vicki and I smiled at each other and at Katherine as she opened her graduation gifts. We laughed as the kids posed with the trees in the background. We were all-in, joined at the collective hip by the two kids who bonded this group.

IN BLENDED FAMILIES—IN MY blended family—I believe there is a subtle but real hierarchy. The stepmom's position is in the background.

Whether it is right or wrong is not the issue. Stepmoms simply need to be prepared for that place—and try to be graceful about it.

I married a man with children. At some point, the question arises: What sort of relationship will you have with the mother of these children? From my very first encounter with Vicki, it was fundamental to me to try to find some answer to this one.

My hope for that relationship was based on simple truths. I wanted her kids to be as happy as they could be, and creating an environment that fostered pleasant, perhaps even enjoyable, experiences for all of us seemed the best way to accomplish this goal.

In reality, my relationship with my husband's ex-wife was then, and is now, a complex one. At times (God forbid!) it cannot help but look a little like those old but common situations from high school—petty jealousies and popularity contests. Ego gets in the way. I desired an equal equation and quickly learned that that is hard to achieve.

I felt challenged by stereotypes and the misconception that a stepmom cannot truly, truly, care about another mom's kids. As a result, stepmoms often have to "prove" themselves. They need to crawl over the silent implication that they have just not done enough. Given enough time. Given enough money. Given enough love. Sometimes it is subtle. Often it is not. Often it is simply not being recognized. I learned from the very first soccer games that it is possible to ignore someone, even when talking with them politely.

I never believed that any of these situations was easy for Vicki. Leaving your kids with another woman, watching them interact, even bond a little, is not fun. But stepmoms, while they may choose to be there now, did not create this situation. Divorce does not occur in one moment. It is a bunch of moments, built up over months or even years. Stepmoms are not a part of these slices of time. And once you are divorced, the likelihood that another person may arrive in your kids' life is reasonable. I am of the opinion that regardless of how or why a person enters into this scenario, they deserve some generosity of spirit for being willing to step into this place and for showing up.

In my observations of other blended families, there were people who despised the ex-spouse and would look at their own husband and wonder, *How could you ever have married her? No wonder it didn't work out! She's nuts.*

There were also camps of people who viewed the traits the second wife did not have in common with the ex-wife as just another validation of why that first marriage dissolved.

In our case, my emotions regarding my stepkids' mom were at times rage, pity, camaraderie, disbelief, and combativeness. It was like one long, curvy mountain road. There were times when I shrugged my shoulders and said, "Whatever," and even a few times when I simply said, "Enough—there will be no more interaction between us."

But for me, it makes more sense to try to value Vicki as my husband's first wife—a woman he chose to have two children with, to love, and to live with. At that point in their lives, way back when, they fell in love, saw a future, and grabbed it. He saw her as a mother for his future children. That is an honor. To see it any differently would make them look like foolish jerks, and that is one thing neither Art nor Vicki can be called.

DURING KATHERINE'S LAST YEAR OF high school, Vicki met a nice guy named Dave. Their interests and personalities were the right mix, and their relationship culminated in the eventual announcement of their engagement. Their union released the kids from some of their worry—Vicki had a companion to hang out with on the weekends for grilled cheese and tomato soup and a strong, welcoming arm to arrive to events on.

Dave's presence changed the dynamic for all of us. Kate knew him better than Ashton, because she was still living at home, but they both liked him and welcomed him into their current world of college and high school thoughts and activities. Dave brought two kids into the relationship, too. I never heard or saw apprehension or reluctance from Kate or Ash regarding their mom's commitment to Dave and his family. They seemed genuinely excited and endorsed the engagement and subsequent marriage. They were happy that their mom was happy.

Dave became a regular participant at the occasions when we gathered, and, slowly, we got to know him, too. From my perspective, it was nice to have an even number of adults when we assembled as a family. Triangles can be difficult to manage. I watched and teased Art later, as he and Dave checked each other out and strutted their individual rooster feathers. Art experienced his first moment of fatherly jealousy when Dave invited Ashton to climb Mount Rainier with him—something Art had hoped to do with his son. But, as the saying goes, guys are different. Emotions do seem to roll off them more easily. And in time, Art and Dave developed a nice, level rapport.

When I heard that Vicki and Dave were engaged, I was cautiously hopeful. I heard that he liked to work with wood and do carpentry as a hobby, and I hoped that he might be able to sand down and smooth out the rough corners that Vicki and I had encountered over the years. There was also a part of me that thought, *Finally, they're going to get it—they will be stepparents, too.* My shoulders lifted up in hopeful anticipation of some change in the air.

But Dave's presence did not altogether alter the way Vicki, her friends, or some folks in the community treated me. The shoulders were still cold and indifferent. Invitations for conversation were still not extended. Nor did it alter the recurring theme of one group in and one group out. Unfortunately, these sentiments seemed dug in pretty deep.

My relationship with Vicki has hit highs and lows over the years. I did and do try. It is also true that there have been many, many times when I have wished I did not have to consider her, her feelings, or her travel plans. But that is not possible. While I understood that I was taking on the dog, the mortgage, the in-laws, et cetera, I also admit that I was not thinking the first Mrs. would be such a constant over the long haul called marriage.

While I may have to deal with the same recurring themes, I have no illusion that I will not always be in a relationship with Vicki, for the simple fact that I love her kids and they love their mother. I made the decision to stick with it. I gear up and walk in. Sometimes I fail. But I will always ask about her and make soup when illness strikes, and I am prepared to have her as a conversation piece, if not a guest, at my dining table. I have chosen to take the position that, as one of the most important people in my stepkids' lives, she is, and always will be, a de facto member of my family.

# 13

⁕

## CHANGES

"**A**RE YOU READY TO GO?" Art asked.

"Yep. Go ahead and take Marlowe down to the car, and I'll be there in a minute."

I closed the door and locked it behind me. It was a bright, beautiful day. A day for squinty eyes and sunglasses. A good day to start a road trip.

We were headed south toward Seattle, crossing the bridge over the Snohomish River and continuing down Highway 522. From the backseat, Marlowe had started another of her many and varied stories for whoever would listen. At the age of four, she was a talker.

We were headed to Queen Anne, a neighborhood in Seattle where Vicki and Dave had recently bought a house and moved to earlier in the summer. As we drove up the hill and turned left down the tree-lined block toward their home, I could see the car being packed with the final suitcases and boxes. They were ready to go. They were driving Katherine to college.

Two years earlier, Art and I had completed this rite of passage with Ashton, opening the car door to his college future. Now it was Vicki's turn.

"Hi!" we all said in unison as we got out of the car.

"Just about ready to go," Vicki said to Art. They stood side by side on the sidewalk, Katherine's parents, discussing the route and the mountain passes that Vicki and Dave would be driving over the next three days on their way to Colorado Springs. The home of Colorado College. My alma mater.

I glanced at Katherine as she threw her pillow and her books for the trip into the backseat. I had really enjoyed my time at CC and carried many good memories of my four years there. I loved being in a different state and a new environment. I loved the mountains, the weather that changed as quickly as it started, and Pikes Peak towering in the background as I walked to class. I was hoping that her experience would meet or surpass my own. Colorado College had been one of many background topics of conversation since I had met Katherine. I still had many friends who lived in Colorado, and she had heard a lot of my college stories over the years. Still, I was pleasantly surprised when she expressed an interest in applying to the school. When her acceptances to CC and the other schools that she had applied to arrived in large envelopes in the mailbox, she and I spent several weeks talking about all the options she could explore as she tried to decide which college to attend. I told her about the block plan at CC—taking one class at a time for three and a half weeks—the snowy winters filled with sunshine, and all the trips she could experience during the four-day break between each block. I took it as a roundabout compliment when she made the decision to go to Colorado—an indirect affirmation from her that maybe I had turned out "okay."

Today, as she waited for the adults surrounding her on the sidewalk to complete the ritual of checking that the boxes would not fall on fast corners and that the oil and gas and tires on the car were shipshape, she looked eager with anticipation. She was more than ready to leave her hometown and start a new chapter. She probably could have kept pace with the car if they had left without her.

Katherine. This girl and I had been through so much over the last five years. We had battled against each other's strong wills and shared deep emotional truths. I had been through so much with her brother, too. And her mother. And now she was off to college. The college that I had attended.

We continued our idle chitchat on the sidewalk as Dave and Art loaded the final boxes into the car. Katherine's high school boyfriend, Pete, hovered nearby. He was the only one on that sidewalk who did not appear keen on the passage of time that was about to commence. He had convinced Vicki and Dave to let him drive in the car until they reached Portland, Oregon, and then he and Kate would have their goodbye and he would grab a Greyhound bus home. Art and I were not expecting their relationship to make it through the next few states after the car crossed the border leaving Oregon.

"Bye-bye, Marl." Kate gave her sister a warm hug. "See you soon."

She turned to me.

"Well. Off you go." I smiled at her. I was loaded with

emotion. More words were not going to be possible. We gave each other what my friends and others often refer to as a "big, fat hug" goodbye.

"Call us when you get there," Art said. "I love you." I watched them say goodbye, and the three of us turned to walk back to our car. I opened the passenger door and slid in.

They started slowly, but in the short time that elapsed between Art's turning the key in the ignition, starting the car, and moving down the street to the stop sign at the end of the block, they were coming fast and furious. Tears. Sobs. The gulping sound when you find it hard to breathe. A true downpour.

It was the emotional release of five years. Five years of immensely high hopes, deep, pitted lows, and everything in between. I cried for a long, long time as Art turned left and drove quietly through downtown Seattle and back to the freeway headed toward home. Each tear, each deep breath, was for every day that had passed from the moment I had met these kids on a long New Year's weekend to this Saturday morning in August as Katherine left for college. Every minute of anguish, happiness, missed communication, and sliver of real connection. I loved her, I loved her brother, and I loved this family. Still did.

I was still all-in.

KATHERINE'S NEW BEGINNING WAS ONE of many in the last nine months. After months of deliberation, Art and I had decided to close our medical business and he had accepted a position as a medical director at a small HMO in Bellevue. In the few years we had had the practice, it had grown ever so slowly, but our enthusiasm for the business had dimmed. Neither Art nor I felt with certainty that a solo practice was a secure financial future for our family. And while Art still enjoyed the actual practice of medicine and seeing patients, I was growing antsy faced with day after day of sitting before a computer, logging in billing codes for insurance companies. While I truly respect those who love that job, it was not making me bound out of bed every day. Art had been talking with other employers for several months, and when the opportunity arose for him to move into the world of health policy issues, he chose to pursue this other passion.

As we reached this decision about the business, the lawsuit that we had filed against his former employer reached mutual resolution days before our trial was set to begin. The months of meeting with lawyers from all sides and sitting opposite the members of his former company were finally over. Like most resolutions, it was a compromise on both sides. By accepting the new job with the HMO, we had bargained away a bit of leverage. But taking the new position had been the right thing for us to do, and we reluctantly accepted the consequences, in the hope that this new job would result in a more confident future. This lawsuit had been a chess game filled with many moves and furrowed eyebrows gazing at the opponent on the other side of the table. To finally close the chapter on this period was like catching a wave from the wake of the boat and flying over the water when you are tubing—absolutely thrilling. It gave our spirits a huge lift. We stepped out of the lawyer's offices happily, with faces up.

Anticipating a trial, we had already arranged for time off

and child care. Instead, we grabbed our passports, dropped Marlowe off at my mom's house and hit the road, driving to Whistler, British Columbia. Just the two of us. Even though the Canadian border is only three hours north of Seattle, there is something about speaking with a border agent and crossing that invisible line into a new country. You have gone somewhere. Away from everything.

We hiked. We slept. We ate. And we returned four days later, ready to turn the proverbial page onto the next chapter.

All of us were looking forward. Katherine to college. Vicki to a new marriage and home. Ashton to a study-abroad program in Costa Rica. Art and I to a new job, more security, and fewer joint obligations.

Now that both of the older kids were eighteen or above, our joint financial commitments were fewer and further apart. The ability to throw that collective pot out the window was in sight, and we welcomed it. It meant fewer discussions about difficult subjects between our households. Fewer reasons to grow irritated.

And with fewer reasons to grow irritated, I held on to my hope that future interactions might result in more enjoyable endings as a group and allow for more fresh air in my own marriage. Whistler had been a welcome reprieve, a time for the two of us not only to eliminate the toxic feelings from the lawsuit but also to expel the bad air that had lingered over the last five years. We talked at length about all the events in the past, how they had affected us, and where we were today. We spoke about our dreams for the next five years. We wanted another baby. We wanted to get out of the debt we had accumulated through our reduced income and our business venture. We wanted time with all of our children that did not center on "big life topics." Balance, a bit of smooth water, and clear weather were our hopes.

IT WAS STRANGE TO GO home and face empty bedrooms. In the period of time that we had been married, there had always been a teenager in our home. With teenage stuff. Makeup left on bathroom countertops, doors closed in such a way that we knew we had to knock to enter, empty plates of food and nasty old juice glasses found under the bed. I already missed it, and it had been only half of one day.

We did what all parents do when their kids leave for college. You strip the sheets off the bed, put them in the washing machine, and remake the bed with an extra fluff to the pillow to get it ready for when they finally come back home. Then you walk into the kitchen, pour yourself a glass of wine, open the refrigerator, and figure out what to make for dinner. It would be a good night for grilled halibut with corn, lime juice, garlic, and avocado salsa with a sprinkle of cilantro on top.

ASHTON AND KATHERINE'S COLLEGE YEARS were filled with transitions and new reveals. The first time home, you notice they are all of a sudden drinking coffee in the morning, with cream and sugar. Each subsequent trip back provides new observations. They have a new piercing and a new way of flicking their hair out of their eyes. They are grown up, but not. They still carry that "it's all about me" attitude, combined with "I now know so much more (than you)."

Each visit home also exposed a new layer in the way they viewed themselves, their world, and even our family. It was a strange combination of being dependent and independent at the same time. Changes were made. The one day at our house and one day at their mom's was retired and sent to child-custody heaven. Ashton and Katherine got to decide where to lay their heads. There were fewer rules and more freedom of thought, along with our observations that some festering and lingering pain was still, sadly, evident.

"I still don't get you, Dad," Ashton said heatedly to Art on a visit home. Ashton had started seeing a counselor at school and, from what we gathered, had been encouraged to confront his dad about the past and express his feelings.

"I really blame you. You made such a mess of things. Why did you do it?"

Our financial situation remained strained. We were slowly eliminating the debts that we had accumulated, but discretionary income was not available. Financial issues continued to be a topic that was difficult to fully explain to Ashton and Kate. Maybe we weren't clear enough, or maybe young adults still cannot fully grasp the big picture.

"I hate the way you talk about money." Ash shook his head at his dad. His feelings were real and honest, but at this point Art was at a crossroads of explanations and answers. There were no new truths to emerge and explain.

"I'm sorry that you feel this way," Art replied with resignation.

"They just don't really understand everything yet," I said to him later. "Maybe one day they will, or maybe they won't. I just don't know. All we can do is love them."

~~~❧~~~

DURING THE SUMMER OF KATHERINE'S sophomore year, we all gathered on the Outer Banks of North Carolina for our next scheduled reunion with Art's side of the family. Warm, sandy wind whipped our hair all around as we all took long walks on the beach, collecting shells and watching the waves. We ate soft-shell crabs, drank beer, and listened to the same stories we had heard at the last reunion.

Katherine joined us midweek. She and I were prickly from the day she arrived, though I could not quite put my finger on why. Certainly, in the two years she had been at school, our relationship had faced some additional tension. Lack of real conversation was a problem. Kate shared less with her dad and me. We sensed we were out of the loop of people she wanted to confide in. She seemed to be distancing herself from our feedback, unless absolutely necessary. She was not forthcoming about school, or about much at all, for that matter. We heard secondhand about huge phone bills to her boyfriend that her mom ended up paying. We sensed she might not be very happy with where she was at college but did not want to tell us. She was entering her twenties, stretching and pushing the boundaries, trying to figure out who she was now and who she was going to be. Sometimes I wondered if I was just a good person for her to try out some of these new concepts on. Could I handle resistance to conversation? How would we deal with not seeing her as much in the summers when she stayed in Seattle with her mom? Maybe it was a test to see if unconditional love was really an option for a stepmom. I don't know.

But from the moment she arrived in North Carolina, she

pushed my buttons, arguing with me and with Art seemingly every time we opened our mouths. She soured noticeably when we asked her anything. She was full of contempt when sitting by us.

We kept trying to get it right, but some connection was misplaced. As I finished my shower on her last day of the reunion, I wondered what I could do to smooth things over before she left later that afternoon. Maybe I could talk to her in the car on the way to the airport. I turned off the sink and heard her talking in the room outside the bathroom door. I looked out and said hi, before noticing she was on the phone. I quickly understood the rhythms of the conversation and knew the person on the other line was her mom.

There was nowhere to go. The cabin was tiny. Standing in the small living area of the cabin, I put my clothes away and folded up the towels as she talked into the rotary phone, sitting on the couch.

Kate moved her legs as I reached under the table to pick up Marlowe's books on the floor.

"Yep, it's been great. Everyone has asked about you. Aunt Trudy told me to tell you how much she misses you," I heard her say to Vicki.

I looked back at her as she watched me walk back into the bathroom. What is it about bathrooms and reunions? I began to slowly simmer, as there was no way to escape this small space and not listen to the rest of the conversation without walking out the door to the outside. It felt like this phone conversation would never stop.

"Gramps is good. He misses you, too. Yep, I'll tell them all you say hi. Bye-bye, Mom. Talk with you when I get home."

I heard the phone being put back into the cradle. Finally, she had hung up and finished this conversation.

I walked back into the living area. Kate looked at me and I looked at her. We both knew.

I would like to say I handled this with maturity and aplomb. I did not. I was hurt and mad, and I told her so. I did not care if Art's family truly missed Vicki; I just did not want to be part of the conversation or near it. I knew by the tone of Kate's voice that these sentiments from her aunt and the rest of her dad's family were very important to her—and I knew that Kate had known I could hear her tell her mom. This conversation, had been, in a slight way, on purpose.

I grabbed my purse and went to get Marlowe. I told Art I was leaving and would not be taking Kate to the airport with him. I had had enough. In the space of that moment, I had had enough of Kate, her dad, and his family. I had hit and crossed my line of patience. I did not look back for it. I left without saying anything, not even goodbye, to Kate. I strapped Marlowe into the convertible rental car, fired it up, and drove down to the end of the point. We stood among the small crowd of people gathered to watch the crew of workers slowly moving the Cape Hatteras lighthouse backward, away from the shoreline eroding around it. The hope was to move the historic landmark to a more protective site.

My own family felt like it needed a more protective site. The ease and balance in our relationships that I so desired seemed just beyond my reach. I still so often felt like the ground below me was eroding. A stable place to sit or stand never lasted very long.

Marlowe and I stood at the end of that point, watching

and walking, for a long, long afternoon. We ate ice cream and dug our feet in the sand. Eventually, I knew I had to return to that small cabin. There was nowhere else to go that day but back.

ASHTON AND KATHERINE WERE STILL upset and hurting, and their feelings were still important to me, but I could not get it right. Art and I continued to spend a great deal of time thinking and talking about the kids and their continued emotional pain. How could we make it better? Was there in fact anything we could do to make it better? I was not so sure. Time away from home does bring much-needed independence, but it can also create distance in true conversation. I felt this distance especially with Ashton. We just were not good phone people together. And e-mails did not seem to work too well, either. They were too short, too polite, too full of no real information. I worried about it. Agitated about it. Talked to Art about it. It still caused me much sadness. And Kate. She and I still circled each other round and round, coming in and going out. Finding real connection and real distance.

ASHTON FINISHED HIS HUMAN-BIOLOGY degree in four years and anticipated later attending medical school. His immediate plan after graduating was to take a year off before applying and travel the world with friends, earn some money, and take a break from academics. In the spring of 1998, we all booked our flights and started our cars to gather in Palo Alto for his graduation weekend of ceremony and celebration.

Ashton's upcoming commencement inspired me to try and think of something—a gift or an event—that I could do for him. I really wanted to try to finish this college experience on a positive note between us—to try to show him again, before he left for another year, that he mattered to me.

"What do you think of a small party?" I asked him. "We could do a barbecue or something."

Several of his high school friends from home were also graduating with his class. They had arrived together, all leaders from a small-town high school, and now they would be walking across another stage to graduate as a group.

"We could invite all your friends from home and their families, along with your friends from school. What do you think?"

"Uh, oh, yeah. That sounds okay," he replied over the phone.

*Great*, I thought. *Let's make this fun.*

I found a cheap bar that would let me rent their outdoor space for next to nothing and planned an easy appetizer social hour with beer and wine. Ashton sent me a list of friends and their families that he wanted to attend and I designed and sent out the invites.

On Friday, the day before the barbecue, Ashton was going over his list of obligations with Art and Vicki for the weekend. I overheard him say he would be at a dinner around 7:00 p.m. on Saturday. I looked over at him. "Are you not coming to the party?"

"Um, well, this other thing is pretty important. I really feel like I should go to it."

I heard my mom's voice in my head.

*Count to ten, Marianne*, she said.

I swallowed my pride.

*Let it go, Marianne*, I said to myself. *Let it go.*

After talking with his dad and his girlfriend, Ashton came to the party for an hour. It was a subdued celebration.

ON SUNDAY MORNING, VICKI, DAVE, Art, Kate, and I sat in the metal bleachers, watching the traditional, elaborate and colorful ceremony down on the stadium field prior to the formal ceremony. It was a parade of students dressed in costumes, with painted faces, running and dancing all over the turf. We all watched later, joined together in the heat of California and in happy anticipation, as Ashton walked across the stage and collected his college diploma. Another milestone. Another family gathering. The final ritual, now a familiar staged event, as each individual family gathered for their own perfect shot in the lingering light of the afternoon.

"HEY, I'VE BEEN THINKING ABOUT what we might want to give to Ash for graduation," I said to Art as he sat down to dinner several months earlier.

"Why don't you take him on a trip, just the two of you? You have some vacation time this summer; maybe you could plan it around that time."

Art looked up from his plate, thinking about it. I knew what he was going to say.

"That's a great idea. Why don't you come, too?"

"Nope, I think it should be just you guys."

Art and Ashton had not taken a trip, a true vacation,

since we had married. As Art and I talked about the possibilities, we both reached the conclusion that it might be a really good thing for the two of them. There had been so many missed communications and spiteful words over the years that a vacation, a break, might just be the thing they needed to point the conversation in a new direction. We did not have a lot of extra money for something exotic or monumental, but we both agreed a trip would be worth it.

Art spent the next several months, in his spare time, researching and planning a weeklong fishing and float trip in the Spatsizi Plateau Wilderness Provincial Park in northern British Columbia. That summer, following the graduation, they flew in to a remote site on a two-engine plane with our Old Blue Canoe attached. Art told me later that as he watched the pilot and his plane fly away, he had a moment of doubt about his plan as he realized the place looked much more remote than had been described. Civilization was out of sight. They gathered their belongings, packed up the canoe, and set off to spend the next week fishing, camping, and repairing their relationship.

A lack of civilization and phones does cause people to turn toward the others they are with and talk with them. Camping has its own rules. You sleep in the tent, side by side, you cook together, and you brush your teeth together. You are close.

Upon their return, I noticed a settling of conflicted spirits. There were smiles, back slaps, and high fives. There were two people retelling the same story about the bull trout and the black bears. There were memories. Good ones.

As Kate's college years went on, she continued to demonstrate her independence and have very strong opinions about everything. She was stubborn and vocal.

"This will be my semester abroad. I don't care what you say—I'm going."

She had fallen in love. True to our prediction, Pete was no longer in the picture album. She had met Ian early in her first year at college, and he was a keeper. A few years older, he had graduated and moved to Sweden to play international hockey. Now, instead of a traditional study abroad, she wanted to go to Sweden and spend some time with him. Neither Art nor I was too excited about this plan.

"But you don't get any school credit. What are you going to do every day?" Art asked her. "I am not enthusiastic about simply sending you to Sweden to sit in a house and then go to hockey games every weekend."

In true blended-family form, she responded, "Well, Mom says it's fine, so I'm going."

You could almost hear the stomping of feet over the phone. It was the end of the discussion. Using one parent's household against the other—a tried-and-true tactic in blended families. We certainly had not thrown that maneuver out the window yet.

Off she went to Sweden.

We were all at a juncture, moving forward but also revisiting some old wounds and hurt feelings. All five of us circled like planets around the word *family*. Still searching for the right rotation, the right gravitational pull, that would allow this to feel natural. Normal. Okay.

At junctures like this, we usually planned a trip. It was time. And so it was decided. "It's time for a family vacation."

The five of us, plus two significant others. We circled the dates on the calendar and counted the days. It had been a long time since we had been together for a period of time that did not include a big seasonal holiday. Ashton was leaving soon to start medical school in New York, and consequently little, if any, vacation would be available for him. Katherine was entering her final year of college, and nowhere in her vocabulary was the idea of coming back to the Northwest anytime soon. We did not have a hockey team in Seattle. It would be quite a while before we all could gather again at the same time, under the same roof.

I threw myself into planning a trip to remember. Our finances were back in relative order, and we all were ready for some fun and adventure. It was funny to think that ten years earlier we had had no such thing as the Internet, but now I could spend all evening checking out sites to explore, finding rivers to cross, and planning menus. I settled on a cabin in the Gallatin Valley, outside Bozeman, Montana. We all arrived after hours of driving—Art, Marlowe, Ashton, his gal, and me from Seattle, and Katherine, Ian, and their pet goldfish from Canada, where they had been visiting Ian's family in Manitoba. We were tired, but the smiles came easily that night as we barbecued hamburgers, husked corn, and poured our first mojitos, overflowing with fresh mint leaves.

Bozeman is a tremendous place, rugged and beautiful. It was ideal for all our ages and interests. Over the next seven days, we floated the Gallatin River in small skiffs, practicing our limited fly-fishing skills. We drove to Yellowstone, Marlowe telling stories the entire way, and spent a full day taking in all its majestic beauty. We rented horses and rode up to a mountain lake for fishing and a picnic. We laughed hysterically as we could barely swing our legs over the saddles to get down, much less walk, after the ride, returning in pitch darkness down the mountain trail. We drove into town to the local bar and watched the kids play pool while Art and I sat on barstools and played cards with Marlowe. We barbecued steaks with Ian's composed blue cheese–butter topping, drank wine, and sat in the hot tub. We played more cards. We laughed. A lot. There was no snark. No tension. No harsh words. This week, our rhythms matched one another's. We circled easily. Our reserve tanks filled up.

On the last night, my emotions overwhelmed me. I choked up and swept away the tears as I raised my glass to this group of five, plus two, who had given me such hope over the week. Hope that we were moving forward, past the pain and silent moments. Past the past.

We packed up the cars. With reluctance, we all went in our different directions, excited for what lay ahead and genuinely looking forward to the next family outing.

KATHERINE GRADUATED A YEAR LATER, in 2001. As I had done with Ash, I planned a party to celebrate her accomplishments, this time at the Garden of the Gods. Her two families, once again, came together. We—Art, Vicki, Vicki's mom, Dave, Ashton, and I—met her friends, walked through my old campus, and capped off the evening with a ceremonial "yard of beer" at the Golden Bee bar. On Sunday morning, she, too, walked across that stage and collected her diploma and bachelor of arts degree.

In a continued tradition, her graduation present was also a trip with her dad. With the same excitement and interest he had shown with Ashton, Art planned a week of salmon fishing in Prince Rupert, on the northern coast of British Columbia. They stayed at a small motel, rose early, and fished through the day. They bonded over their successful catch of halibut and salmon and the laughter and kidding only your own kid can hand out while watching her dad get seasick for two long hours on a very small boat.

Their return was also accompanied by a flurry of smiles and high fives, and a carload of flash-frozen salmon and halibut.

Those first years after your kids leave the house are significant in many dimensions. Everyone adjusts to new living arrangements, fewer faces around the dinner table, and new ways of relating and communicating. No one knows for sure how those adjustments will end up. Biological parents assume it is the next rite of passage before their kids hit full adulthood, a pass-through to the next phase of life.

For us—for me—there were different nuances. It was a time when my stepkids had more freedom, without their dad looking over their shoulders to decide what, if any, kind of relationship they would have with me.

It was a period of just waiting. Strangely, it felt similar to the way I make "clean-the-fridge soup"—with a little bit of everything you can find in the refrigerator thrown in. There are the basics—onion, garlic, carrots, and celery—but then just pile it on and clean out the vegetable drawers. Add stock and a little bit of wine. If you are in the mood for some meat, add bacon or hot Italian sausage. Add a lot of salt and pepper and a rind of parmesan. Let it sit.

In that period of time after Katherine and Ashton left home, we threw in all the emotions and the remaining pain. We tossed in laughter and included some really good memories. We added Ian—a very funny and welcome addition.

Yet I could no more predict now than I could in the beginning whether the pain would lessen, the relationships would grow stronger, and all of the planets would align. All I could do was let it sit and wait it out.

# 14

## OUR FAMILIES (HERS)

"I'M SO GLAD MY KIDS got to meet your kids. I wanted them to know that some members of his family were good, decent people."

Art and I had already been married for twelve years when one of Vicki's siblings made this statement to one of Art's siblings at a family celebration. It was one of those inevitable occasions that occur within blended families where all the players intersect—Art's family, Vicki's family, and, in this case, a few members of my family.

It is hard to know what to make of this remark. It brings up many reactions. But the comment's history goes back to the beginning, when two people married and a blended family was created. It begs the question, what do you do with the family of your stepkids' mother when you marry and become the next family? There is no easy answer to this one. As with so much of this blended meal, there are a lot of ways to stir this pot.

In my reality, it was pretty hard to ignore Vicki's family. They remained related to the kids. Over the years, there were family reunions and celebrations of life's events. Aunts, uncles, and cousins came up in conversations. They visited Seattle, and the kids visited them in their hometowns. Their names, already embedded in Art's life history, became familiar to me.

In the midst of this jumble were the remnants of a relationship between all the former relatives. The ex-spouse was linked to them in an ex-spouse kind of way. Memories existed. Art was still the brother-in-law who talked at length about growing tomatoes. He was still the uncle who had swung his nephew up on his shoulders and hiked up the hill. There was just a two-letter difference in his description now—*ex*.

VICKI'S FAMILY, LIKE ART'S, IS a big group, all living in different states. After Art and Vicki separated and divorced, there were no continued conversations or phone calls between Art and his former in-laws. Instead, there were whispers in the wind chimes, pictures left in ruin, and rumors in the walls. We never saw them clearly; they were more like little critters scampering around undercover.

When Art's former relatives visited Vicki, they scheduled no lunches to catch up with him; in fact, they had no interaction whatsoever, unless by coincidence at a soccer game. Their reserved air was in direct contrast with the manner in which Art's family treated Vicki.

Now, I am not forgetting that there were some mighty hurt feelings on Vicki's side. The marriage had ended badly and painfully. I do get it. At a minimum, it was awkward and uncomfortable. And we were not at a minimum.

But is this really the way these things have to go? Choosing sides, choosing battle lines, again, seemingly forgetting that there are small people involved? What does it do to a kid's head to see one side of a family treat their father as invisible, lower than dirt, while their mother is welcomed, hugged, and invited to break bread? What residue remains? Can it ever be wiped clean? Does this theme have to be fueled and blown on for all the many years to follow?

As integral as the mother is, the dad remains integral, too. Should Art not have been greeted or asked about as a part of his kids' lives? Was he not relevant? And once their sister was born, was she ever inquired about? Or was she, too, banished from the kids' reality when they were with their mom's family?

Art's reaction to these frozen overtures was mixed. In the first years, his biggest concern was Ashton and Katherine. What did they see? What did they feel? Beyond that, Art knew he was not going to change the mind or the behavior of his former relatives. He did not even try. He felt their silent wrath. When standing beside them, he sensed, in the way they looked at him, that they believed he was the sole person at fault for the demise of his marriage to Vicki. The guilt that he already carried for his part in the breakup was underlined and highlighted in the brief conversations he had with them. But he stood up straight and took it in the gut.

The years ticked by, and even these brief interactions

with Vicki's family became less frequent, though they never went away altogether.

In our reality, and, I think, in most blended families, events to which we would all be invited continued to transpire. That summer, twelve years in, both Ashton and Katherine had found the loves whom they chose to commit to—to marry with open hearts and true joy, in two ceremonies to be shared with all the people they loved.

At the wedding celebration for my stepdaughter, it almost seemed as if we had put the past aside, finally. Laughter and good tidings among all families occurred. But around the corner at my stepson's wedding, it was the total opposite. There were blank looks, absent conversation, and jockeying for family nearness.

And then, out of the blue, this sentiment was spoken out loud: "How nice that there are a few good, moral people in your clan."

Boorish behavior? Maybe. Regardless, these comments and grudges leave a stain.

I can pull out a tablecloth, used only for special events, and see the remnants of a red-wine spill from some dinner past. The dry cleaner did their best, but the shadow of that wine spill remains, reminding me of that specific occasion. Words are no different. And if this was the sentiment being expressed twelve years in, what was said in the previous years?

One of the problems stems from the opening sentiment of my stepchildren's relative: our situation was not viewed as an equilateral triangle. One side was still seen as the "poor victim" and the other side as the "big asshole." And the third side, whether it was just me or additional members of my family, was left standing somewhere, several steps back, from all these interactions. Sometimes acknowledged. Sometimes not.

I'll be straight: I did not give ten minutes' worth of thoughts, glances, or overwhelming interest to my husband-to-be's former family prior to our marriage. I was stupid and simply not realistic. Interactions, love, family time, and family community continue to thrive, as they should.

When I did begin to incorporate Vicki's family into my blended-family awareness, I did not imagine that the interactions would feel one-sided, that "our side" would be considered less-than. I used to be pretty good at mathematical equations, and the less-than and greater-than signs are a fitting analogy for blended families. At least mine. The equal sign was not on the page.

It was the same old themes once again rising to the surface.

However, what members of both the family and the community overlook is that Art and Vicki will always have a connection. Divorce does not change that fact. They are bonded by their children and a distant love that created those beautiful human beings. I have witnessed, over the years, Art and Vicki talking comfortably over the sink, washing dishes side by side, after a dinner party at Katherine's. I have seen them commiserate, as only co-parents can, over their joint concern for one of their children. No matter how many years go by or how many additional people are brought into their households, this bond exists.

Unfortunately, I have also observed the ability to push aside that notion of a continual bond when it is not convenient. Somewhere between washing the dishes and adding the old family and friends to that mix, the link becomes hidden in the shadows, pushed to the side by stereotypes and other people's expectations of how one should respond to an "ex" and their new partner.

The need to keep up appearances—that one side is a victim and the other side is the ultimate loser—seems to override all other options.

Even twelve years in, some folks in my community carried on with these themes. Attending a political caucus event, I approached a group standing in conversation, waiting for the voting to commence.

"Hey." I smiled at the parent of one of Marlowe's classmates. "How are you?"

I smiled at the rest of the party of five adults. My eyes traveled with my voice, acknowledging the small group of people. The lack of eye contact from the one standing directly across from me was obvious. She did not return my hello. I shook my head. *Really?* I wondered.

When the phone rang the next day, I was caught by surprise when I realized her husband was on the other end of the line.

"How are you?" he started. "What a great evening it was last night. Well, you know we go way back ..."

I listened as he talked about our connections and how I had given each year to the charity on whose behalf he was calling. I struggled to stay upbeat in the conversation. I liked the charity. But, really, you're going to say we go "so far" back? On a positive note? The conversation felt filled with hypocrisy.

"So," he continued, "how much would you and Art like to contribute this year?"

He was right. In fact, we did go way back. I had welcomed these people to my home for dinner. They had kids Marlowe's age who participated in the same events. I had seen them repeatedly around town at school, athletic events, and the gym. When he had first solicited me, one of the reasons I had given a donation was that I hoped we could be more than acquaintances. But they were also in Vicki's circle. And clearly, based on my greeting the night before, there was still a dividing line between us. Appearances needed to be kept.

I probably stepped even further away from a relationship when I told him that Art and I were rethinking our charitable donations for the year.

"I'm not going to be able to donate right now," I said into the phone.

In a strange coincidence, another friend of Vicki's called later that week, also soliciting funds for a local cause. The amount she wanted was significant. She hoped that she and her husband, once a good friend of Art's, could meet with us to discuss the proposal. Once again, I found myself falling back into that space of hoping and wishing that this was a sign of a change in attitude, that it was in fact a gesture of goodwill. But it was not. The conversation got clouded when she expressed her interest in having her family meet only with Art—"for old times' sake"—and that if it was inconvenient for me, I really did not need to be there.

I hoped that by then my skin would have grown tough, immune to these slights, but I still felt the sting. Whether I was standing alone and ignored in an old farmhouse, brushed by at a community event, or asked to donate by people who were not really interested in talking to me at other times, these snubs bugged me.

"Do you think they're ever going to just move on?" I asked Art at dinner one night.

"I don't know what to tell you. You still seem to be the collateral damage for my decisions."

"I'm sorry."

I HAVE SEEN BLENDED FAMILIES—mine and others—stuck in this place where "the other side" is intent on keeping up the appearances that one side is good and the other side is not. For some reason, it seems that the dad is more often the one who is kept at bay, banished from the groups and relationships that he once frequented. I have not seen instances in which this stance has been helpful to anyone, but I have seen it cause a great deal of pain and damage.

It hurts the kids who call him Dad. They are not blind to the changes in overtures. I often wondered if the kids of these people who turned from Art and me, consciously or unconsciously, copied their parents' opinions and ended up engaging in similar behavior toward our family. Either way, I think it put Ashton and Katherine in an uncomfortable and unnecessary position.

This kind of behavior also hurts the stepmom. People's need to keep up appearances, to stretch out the theme that a second marriage is somehow tainted, not equal to the first one, creates a cloud over your own relationship, whooshing and shifting into the shape of a question mark.

Early on in my marriage to Art, I created a silly goal for myself to hold out longer in my marriage than his union to Vicki had lasted. I told myself how dumb this objective was—it wasn't as if I were trying to make the Ironman circuit or run my first marathon—but it stuck in my head. I silently patted myself on the back, put that medal around my neck, when we reached that finish line. Later, another stepmom, without knowing my own goal and with the same level of shy embarrassment, told me she had set out to do the same thing herself: she wanted to last longer than her husband's first wife. We laughed in camaraderie with each other.

It was as if by making it longer, surpassing the length of our husbands' first marriages, we would get the validation we desired and that we knew we deserved. It would authenticate our presence to the kids involved, the relatives who cried foul, and the community that turned its back. I hope this stepmom makes her goal, too. I will share my medal.

# 15

OUR KIDS

$\mathcal{K}$IDS. IT WOULDN'T BE A blended family without them, right?

Art and I had an ongoing conversation about kids from the very beginning, and that topic has continued to be an ongoing line of discussion throughout our entire marriage. At first, we talked about his two—Ashton and Katherine. A lot. He told me birth tales. The overwhelming emotion he felt when they were born. What he looked forward to doing with them now. He bragged about their athletic abilities and intelligence. He described their personalities. He spoke of character traits they demonstrated—strong qualities that showed up without advance notice and seemingly from out of the blue.

He reminisced about his history with them. Ice skating with the first child on the morning of the second's birth. Canoe adventures and mishaps with his daughter and her friend that bordered on frightening. The immediate shock of fear when his son fell off the deck. The joy of reading the illustrated *Hobbit* to them every night at bedtime.

Art talked with candor about the immense hurt that his separation from their mom caused them. He described his worst day: sitting down to tell them. He described the anguish he witnessed and his own pain about his role in that grief. And he always spoke very frankly about his overwhelming love for them.

These stories were a central part of our getting-to-know-each-other conversations over food, during walks, and while driving. His desire to discuss his children was then, and is now, one of his most attractive qualities.

When we dated, Art easily understood that I was quite comfortable embracing his children. He also knew I wanted more. On my list of marriage desires, kids were close to the top, and if Art was going to stick with me, it was part of the contract.

Our philosophy, from the first moment of my pregnancy and through Marlowe's subsequent birth, was not complicated. She was a new sister, an equal member of the family. Her needs and desires would not outweigh those of the first two kids, nor would their needs and desires outweigh hers. We were all-in, one family unit. Period.

On paper, that philosophy looked pretty good. I think it even worked ... most of the time. Marlowe was as inquisitive as most kids are, and she had the gift of a huge imagination. She rolled with the facts of her life. When she was young, she adapted, as small kids do. Her brother and sister had another mother. They all had the same dad. Every other day, Ashton and Katherine went and stayed at another house with their mom. They had a dog over there, too. And a ferret. They had cool older friends, especially Katherine's boyfriends. They were fun.

This was her normal.

She did ask questions.

"Where do babies come from?"

"Why is grass green?"

"Why do I have to take a nap?"

Somewhere along the way, she learned about the terms "half-sister" and "half-brother," but not from me.

My comments, statements, or introductions never went, "This is your half-sister ..." It was simply "This is your sister. This is your brother."

Marlowe was one of those small kids who had to have the correct answer—she had been told never to lie—and a few times she did try to "correct" us. My response was always the same.

"Half-sister? Which half is your sister? Doesn't the blood circulate throughout the entire body? So which half is yours?"

She thought seriously about that concept, her little brain whirling vigorously as she imagined blood racing through the body, and then she usually smiled and moved on to the next important life topic: "How do birds fly?"

Our philosophy—one family, all-in—worked pretty well, with some notable exceptions. When you do not live under the same roof day in and day out, not to mention when there is a significant age gap between siblings, the kids do not experience the same things: the shared family history, the same growing-up stuff.

Logistically, some typical elements are not possible. The built-in babysitter everyone joked about with me was not likely. I would not have asked Katherine or Ashton to babysit on a night or weekend when they were at their mom's house.

Blended families do not always take vacations, weekend trips, or even singular adventures together, either. The shared spontaneous laughter, the adrenaline rush of all being in the same boat floating down the rapids, the horrible restaurant with the really strange waitress you all found on that remote highway—these events are not always experienced communally. And the subsequent narrative about these occasions does not translate into a mutual emotional experience.

But we rallied. We carved pumpkins and made snowmen. We read books with each other. We did puzzles. We ate together as often as possible. We compromised naps to go pick up our sister or brother. We turned the volume down during the scary movie so our little sister could sleep. We operated as a family as best we could.

Like all good mothers, I felt guilty about them all. I felt guilty that I spent so much time worrying about my stepkids' happiness that I wondered if I was neglecting the last child. I worried that Marlowe was able to experience things that the first two had not, simply because of their dad's different maturity and place in life. Mixed in with the laugh lines on my face is a map of all this guilt and worry.

After I had Marlowe, some people commented, "Isn't it great to finally have a daughter of your own now?" My reality was very different. It was great to have a baby. It was equally great to have two daughters. It was great to have a son. I loved them all.

As the two older kids grew, graduated from high school, and left for college and more independent lives, a lot of things in our family life naturally changed. But one status—sister, sister, brother (not half, full, full)—was then, and continues today, to be my mantra and my wish for them.

Art and I hoped to have at least one more child, but nature had some other ideas and a younger sibling turned out not to be in our cards. I do think it would have been nice for Marlowe to have some siblings closer in age, but she does not. That is life. And as all three kids have grown older, their relationships as siblings are no different than the relationships I have with my brother and sister. It is up to them, as independent people, to decide how best to forge ahead with communication, closeness, and love.

I APPROACHED BEING A BIOLOGICAL parent much the same way I entered step-parenting. One day you don't have kids, and the next day you do. And I assumed all these kids would like me, though *assumed* is not really the right word. In many ways, I just sort of expected it. Not expected as in I deserved it, but expected it the way I knew the sun would rise and set and the moon would shine.

There has never been a day when I have wondered whether my biological child likes me. There have been many days, stretching out to months in a row, when I have wondered if my stepkids do.

And you know what? They don't have to. Your stepchildren do not have to like you—ever. They do not have to acknowledge you, either. I have not heard a lot of people say this out loud. No one really goes there. It is not a really positive thought.

And I suppose the reverse is true. You do not have to like your stepchildren. Except if you love their dad. Because not liking his kids makes life full of additional challenges. And who wants a bunch of challenges beyond what life is already going to throw at you anyway? I did not.

The initial days and months with one's stepkids are like any new relationship. You're in a honeymoon period. You try. You are polite, friendly, and at times just a little too saccharine-sweet. Like most honeymoons, this time period ends quickly. It is too hard to keep up that appearance. Your stepkids soon realize that you, too, sometimes leave your socks on the floor and that you do not like to wash windows any more than they do.

As months and years go by, the interactions between all of you become more real, more organic. "Trying" to be nice and friendly becomes something else, hopefully a more natural state of being. With luck, it is unforced and free of the creaky hinges that opened the door to the relationship in the beginning.

With luck.

Sooner or later, they will find out that you have an ugly side, too. A side that gets angry and frustrated and shouts or cries and even swears. Ideally, it does not show up too early in the relationship.

There were times over the years when I pushed or pulled at my stepkids. I asked them for things—words and emotions—that I should never have asked for. At different points in time, I wanted some endorsement from them and I asked for it, wondering if they ever really noticed me.

"Ash, what *do* you really think of me? Even you have to admit my actions over the years have been more like a mom's than a friend's." I stood there, waiting, imploring him to say something.

Sheepishly, he shuffled, looked everywhere but at me.

"Sure, Mar," he said, gazing downward, the answer falling to the floor.

There I stood, at my lowest, self-esteem swallowed up by some personal tornado, searching for where I belonged. I did this when I was at the end, skin turned inside out and prickly, standing on tiptoe on that thin string between being reasonable and being unreasonable. I am not proud of it. In fact, I am ashamed of these interactions. I am truly sorry.

STEPMOMS HAVE A BASKET OF words available for them to choose from in their relationship with their stepkids. One of them is *benevolence*. A stepmom has a choice to be or not to be benevolent. Do you write that card, extend that invitation, make that phone call—for your sake and/or for the sake of your husband's love of his children? Do you make that effort when that emotion is not reciprocated?

You try. It is draining. You are not a saint. But you like the idea of saints, and so you try again. And you explode once every year (okay, maybe twice) in frustration and hurt feelings, and then you sit up and try all over again.

These situations put the dad between many rocks and hard places as he tries to navigate the different people and their emotional positions. It is a river full of miscommunication, real feelings, and naked truth. His canoe gets stuck several times along the way, but he paddles on, hoping for a resolution.

I do not have good answers to this complex scenario. Feelings on all sides are justified, real, and true. I know many stepmoms who have struggled with these circumstances. The stakes are high. The choice of giving without receiving, while it looks good on paper, is very, very difficult sometimes.

There. Is. Just. So. Much. Emotion.

I remember a movie with Catherine Zeta-Jones and Sean Connery in which, in their attempt to steal a priceless piece of art, they enter a room with an intricate web of lasers. Zeta-Jones must step, leap, slide, and twirl like a dancer to get to the podium holding the treasure without setting off any alarms. This is a classic stepmom dance. You pivot, duck, and dodge around all the beams that factor into this complex dynamic of like, love, and allegiance.

It is within these intricate moves that blended marriages lose air. It is an exhausting dance. Stepmoms often turn to their husbands—the fathers of these kids—and expect them to do something, anything, to make this right, to fix it, but there is not much that dads can do. As a consequence, it is easy to fall into the trap of walking away from each other emotionally. Neither one of you feels supported by the other person. You both feel alone. There is a tendency to throw in a bunch of other issues, too, so you forget what made you feel alone in the first place. Blame is tossed everywhere, when in fact there is no one to scapegoat.

Art and I have fallen into this trap often. We have felt far apart from each other and alone. It has taken us a long time to learn to avoid that pitfall or, at a minimum, to recognize when the other person is falling into that hole and to quickly stick out our hand to pull them out.

One thing that I have learned is that stepmoms have to be really secure and confident and hold themselves in high esteem. All the time. I was terrible at this. There were times over the years when I let the cracks of self-doubt and shyness get wider, and when recognition, either from my community or from my stepkids was absent, I got so sad that these feelings overwhelmed me and rattled my old chains of depression and disillusionment.

IF I HAD FIVE WORDS I could include as absolutely necessary in my basket of a blended-family narrative to share with other stepmoms and the family they marry, they would be *generosity, acknowledgment, understanding, recognition,* and *forgiveness.* Over the years, I have come back to all of these words. I have tried to use them as my "go-to" map. I have touched them, spoken them, and felt them. My hope was that these words and their meanings would be my guide to better relationships and conversations.

Many times they succeeded. But oftentimes, the fatigue factor inherent in blended families prevents success. The effort of using these words and their definitions gets hidden under the bedsheets and forgotten in the closet. They are too often replaced by *absenteeism, insincerity, blindness, misunderstanding,* and *judgment.*

The art of conversing with truth and honesty is hard enough for traditional families. If you add the spice of a blended family, those same conversations can be that much more difficult. There is no blood that ties you. The conversation must hold together on its own merit and, hopefully, contain the themes in my basket.

Art and I have not stopped talking about our three kids. We discuss their many accomplishments. We deliberate with concern if they seem to be suffering. We keep striving to get the conversations right between us and with the three of them.

For myself, I keep carrying my basket on my hip, a reminder that its contents continue to be a necessity and a guide for all my travels—as both stepmom and non-stepmom.

# 16

## MARRIAGE

"Let's take a picture of just us," she said.

I turned and looked back around. The smiling mom stood waving her children in, one on each side, and then posed, waiting for the camera to click, snapping the picture of "just them." Her new husband, whom I had met earlier, was over on the left, standing next to a tree in the shade, a silent observer in the background.

From the expression on his face, I could not gauge what his feelings about the scene before him were, but I remembered my own feelings about these moments. They were uncomfortable. I'd stand there, smiling, trying not to fidget, and feeling a tad self-conscious. Despite my outward smile and demeanor, these incidents always made me feel like a lone and awkward bystander, literally standing by, not a member of that family posing to the left.

No matter how independent I was, how confident I felt, this picture of a family was a thorny issue. I told Art early on how I felt about this type of rebuff, and he remained extremely sensitive to my feelings about it. I did not mind if my stepkids wanted or asked for a picture alone with their dad. In fact, I really understand and empathize with any kid's desire to have a picture with their biological parent, but if I am standing there at the party, do not ask me to step out of the frame. Wait until you are alone, and then snap away. There has not been an occasion in my memory when I would have asked for a picture of just Art, Marlowe, and me if Ashton and Katherine were available to be included.

On the surface, the picture of a family is the two adults and their offspring. Below the surface, in a blended family, it is another matter. No matter how hard I tried to steer away from it, no matter how often I emphasized we were all-in, one unit, there have been repeated moments over the years when the portrait of my family has felt compartmentalized.

I think this tendency to compartmentalize is another of the many hurdles a blended family faces. An atmosphere of separateness corrodes the very thing you are trying to create: a family. Part of being a family is being there, being an observer, either in person or in later shared confidences, of the laughter, the anger, the joy. It helps you put together the whole puzzle of why someone is feeling a certain way, why they might have a certain opinion. It is inclusive.

However, in many instances, blended families can feel like a big apartment complex with rooms for every scenario, separating and dividing. In my family, there is a room for Ashton, Katherine, and their mom. There is another floor of rooms when they are visiting with Vicki's family. Kate and Ash are in a separate room when they are not on the same holiday with my family. I am not in the same compartment when they are alone with their dad, bonding on a much-needed trip. Kate and Ashton are in a different room when they leave home and Marlowe, Art, and I carry on with our life. All these different rooms are hard to keep up.

And if you are not very careful, this compartmentalization can create some difficult environments. The doors are too often left closed, the ones on the outside never knowing the activities and voices of the interior. I have found myself feeling as if I were tiptoeing quietly and ever-so-carefully by each door, trying to be sensitive to everyone, not wanting to barge in on the privacy of the other rooms but also not wanting to behave as if I did not care about the activities in that place. It is a fine line to maintain.

There can also be a propensity for rooms to break into twos or threes, creating an atmosphere where certain people become the outsider looking in. I know what it is like to stand in that position, watching Art, Katherine, and Ashton. I believe that Katherine and Ashton have felt this way when they were not a part of my family's activities. I even believe that Marlowe has felt this way when observing Kate and Ashton. These situations do nothing but create a dusty mess of frustration and loneliness.

There have been very few times when I have referred to Katherine and Ashton as Art's kids, rather than ours. I am not sure how Ashton and Katherine felt about my referring to them that way, or how they felt when I said I had three kids, not just one, but for me it was the most inclusive, the best, way to, again, let them see and hear my commitment to them.

But I will concede that there are times when they *are* only his kids. The three of them have an innate rhythm born of a lifelong relationship. They have a unique way of communicating that is different if I am there in the conversation or even in the same room. Instances arise in which Art is the only one who can talk with them, reason with them, or simply be there, be present, for them.

In the first years of our marriage, it had to be Art who talked to Katherine and Ashton about Vicki. When Ashton finally felt the freedom to express his feelings, there was no one but Art who could step in and talk it through with him. Only Art, as her father, could listen and offer a certain type of emotional support to Katherine that she needed and deserved.

I supported and even, at times, created space for these conversations to take place. Unfortunately, this space can also breed an environment of us versus you, stepmom versus the others. It may be real and it may be imaginary, but no matter how many times I said, "Nah, that's not what's going on," that feeling that there is a line, and that you are on the other side of it, is hard to shake off sometimes.

I recall a phone conversation that Art had with his sister one night in the first years of our marriage. After he hung up with her, he walked back into the solarium and sat down.

"How is she doing?" I asked him. I was watering the magenta bougainvillea that I had been coaxing to survive and grow in the sun-drenched room.

"She's doing fine. It's been cold there."

"So, what were her thoughts?"

Art had been talking with her and explaining all the ups and downs we were having with Kate and Ash and Vicki.

"She told me to make sure you knew that I was on your side."

Sides. That is the crux. The kids wanted and needed their dad on their side, to have their back. I expected and needed Art to be on my side, to be my partner. He insisted that he was on everyone's side, but it was hard to see and hard for him to communicate. Without really being able to put our finger on what it was, each of us felt like some "thing" was missing. The trap was set, and once we stepped into it, it was hard to get out of without a lot of effort.

Compartmentalization and maintaining sides. Fractures and splinters. These tendencies have presented themselves in my blended family over the years. They do not help foster a home.

Blended-family marriages have a very high divorce rate. This is not a surprise to me. I always shied away from looking up the exact percentage of the failure rate. I did not want to plant a number in my head, give myself a reason to say, *If all those people can't make it work, how are we going to?*

There are many legitimate reasons why blended marriages are difficult, but I do not believe the kids are one of them. I think it boils down to a state of feeling alone and isolated, of not being in a partnership. When Art and I dated and grew committed, we were one. One step. One future. One vision. I looked forward to moving on in life with that one person who could see every side of me, the individual who stood there, arms open, to receive the trust that I gave and carried the weaknesses that I showed him. The person who understood and accepted all of my exposed vulnerabilities.

But we lost sight of each other early on in our marriage. We tried to balance everyone's pain and happiness and left each other to dance by ourselves. I can remember looking across the room one night, fire crackling away in the fireplace, and wondering about him, *Who are you? Where did that guy Art go?*

We started with an allegiance to each other, an invisible but magical silk line wrapped tightly around the other person's heart. I think that we both thought that our attachment was so strong, it could hold out. But then it frayed with the first signs of doubt that the other person was not on our side anymore, when the tension between us and Vicki or the community or the kids was so taut that I walked away or Art walked away. Our grip on that silk line slipped, little by little.

And one afternoon or evening, you find yourself standing by yourself. And when you feel all alone, it is easy to ask the question *What is the point? Of this partnership? Of this marriage? You did not get married to feel even more alone than you did when you were single.*

When I was young, I used to have a bad dream that began with my sitting in an oversize chair in a strange room. I would be waiting, looking around the room, feeling like someone else was in the room, too, and suddenly the chair would start to spin, beginning very slowly but finally reaching an uncontrollable speed. Round and round the chair would go, my feet flying off the ground, the colors in the room blinding black, then isolated white. I would wake up with a start, looking quickly around my bedroom for all the people who I felt sure were in that spinning room with me, only to find it empty. Spinning, out of control, and empty—that was what feeling singular and alone in a marriage felt like to me. It was a feeling that would come and go for many, many years.

BY THE TIME ASHTON AND Katherine had gotten married and created their own spaces for love and happiness, the vision I had for my own home was waning. I still enjoyed the nonstop view and the animal activity from the solarium, but I was struggling to see a future of joy or even contentment in the surrounding area. I had been feeling that chair spin for too long. I was worn down, and whereas I had always been able to find some new energy to step out with optimism, I was having trouble keeping that optimism alive. I felt like I was in retreat—from the town, from the hopes that I had for our house, and even from myself. As much as Art loved this house on a hill—a house where I had invested so much, where everyone had a room and everyone had a memory—it no longer felt like a place I could call home.

So Art and I began a discussion about leaving. We were cautious. Moving from one place to another had to be about more than just moving from one place to another. At the same time, overly high expectations could result in big disappointments.

"Are you okay with this?" I asked him. I stirred the vegetables I was sautéing on the stove and turned to him.

"Yes. I think this is what we need to do." He smiled gamely, his can-do spirit ready for action.

"It isn't working here. We need a change."

We sat at the table, finishing our wine, and planned for the next year.

The timing fit. Marlowe was in her last year of middle school and would be moving into high school in the fall. The three of us started talking and narrowed our search to five schools within a fifty-mile radius. With happy anticipation, Marlowe picked a school in downtown Seattle that she thought would be a good place to start her next academic adventure.

At the end of the summer, carrying some sadness and some guilt that all three kids blamed me for "making" Art leave, I packed up the dishes, cleaned out the refrigerator, and turned off the lights.

We moved to a rental in Seattle, three dogs, three people, and that sense of anxious excitement that comes when you're heading off to a new experience. That first weekend I found my pie plate, flour, and sugar and rolled out the dough with my grandmother Helen's old rolling pin. I cut rhubarb, rinsed strawberries, and made pie.

Tried and true. It comes bubbling out of the oven and makes the house smell nice. A good slice of pie makes you feel like you want to linger a little longer. It was hope. Hope that this change would be the cleansing breath our marriage needed, that I needed, that our entire family needed.

We settled in that week, getting used to the new sounds outside our windows. We had neighbors we could actually hear talk. There were kids who played and laughed on the school grounds across the street. We walked down the block to have coffee and to buy milk. We encouraged our three dogs to like this new thing called a leash and began walking them every day through our new neighborhood.

Fall, my favorite season, was in the air. The leaves turned and started collecting on the ground. It was brisk. At night, we could smell the first fires being lit in the wood-burning fireplaces. Fall is a time of hibernation, but for me it has also been a time for collecting oneself. It often feels like my new year. A time to set some new goals. A time to close the door at the end of the day and subtly gather those around you with smells from the kitchen and a warm, cozy room and, without any grand gesture, simply enjoy the camaraderie of being together. That is what we did.

ONE OF ART'S FAVORITE BOOKS and movies is *The Princess Bride*. We have watched it too many times to count. As a consequence, every time I think of my marriage with Art, it always sounds like *mawwage*. It is what brings us together in all its strangeness and complexity.

Art and I have talked of ending our marriage on numerous occasions over the many years we have been together. We have fought like crazy and feral cats, had evenings when we spoke no words to each other and gone to bed seething with anger. We have sat on numerous chairs and couches in counseling offices and listened to the advice of experts and friends. I have wept in despair. He has howled in frustration. We have tested on a repeated basis our level of commitment to each other.

We have also spent the night under a makeshift Moroccan tent on the deck of the house on the hill, listening to the bats swoosh above us. We have sat in the sweet silence of not having to say anything as we watched the sun go down over the Oregon coast while driving north on Highway 1. We have slurped oysters straight from the shell, wrestled over the last bite of *huevos rancheros*, and bit with joint relish into the rarest, juiciest steaks. We have hiked, ridden horses, skinny-dipped, gone to the theater, laughed over movies, and been swept away by great concerts.

I have no marital advice for blended families. Each one is different. In my case, it comes down to one simple thing: no matter how angry I have been, no matter how many steps I have taken toward the front door, I cannot forget the fact that at the end of the day, Art is still the guy whom I look for when I want some question resolved or have some problem to sort out, or simply to hold me when I am feeling my worst. He is the guy I want to share my triumphs with, who always eats my food, and who usually lets me sing in the car.

Our marriage, like my stepmom experience, has been a big bowl of just about everything a person could imagine. We have churned, kneaded, sat, and risen to whatever the occasion has demanded of us. It has not always been pretty or easy, but we still stand side by side and we still sleep together night after night.

# Epilogue

❧

## BETWEEN THE LINES

*T*HERE ARE NIGHTS WHEN, IF the breeze blows just right, softly and whispering a caress of relief, I can see my mom, throwing a white bed sheet up into the air, smoothing it flat with her hand as it falls, and tucking in the corners tightly around the rectangular cushion. She adds soft cotton blankets and a big, fluffy comforter. Last, she places a pillow at the top of this makeshift space. She is making the bed for my brother Robert on the blue lounge seat on the back porch of our old, red house. The porch faces west, looking out to the lake and even farther, to the dark trees on the point of land across from her home.

This outside porch is where Robert wanted to sleep until the end of his last September, when the breeze turned into wind and became too cold for outdoor slumber. Mom would light the lamp so he could read, touch him gently on the arm or his forehead, and say good night.

I tried to do this for my blended family. I threw the sheet

up into the air and tried to make everything warm, loving, and comfortable. It is just what I do. I was not "trying" to be their mother or their stepmother. I was simply trying to give; I am a caregiver. Always have been. In high school, my friends called me Mother Hen.

I have always liked a good collage. The interesting ones reveal bits and parts of overlapping stories. The longer you gaze at the picture, even years later, additional stories come to light, hidden behind the first impression. When I think back on the past twenty-odd years of my married life, I see it as a big medley that includes colors, music, accusations, fear, joy, resentment, love, food, animals, skies, birds, and imbalance, among other things. All these elements overlap and bump into each other. The colors and shapes blur together, masking strong and complex emotions. They circle around and around and come back to the word *family*.

Deep down in my inner corners is this need for, this desire for, a family. It is my food and drink. I thought about it, fought for it, needed it. I believe it is the one ingredient that makes you defend your ground, climb mountains, and step into dark caves without a headlamp. These individuals—the man I married, the two kids whom I embraced, and the child we created—will make me stand when I want to fall, and make me collapse when I want to stand. A big chunk of my identity is twisted around and around these folks.

I got married for the same reason many people get married: I fell deeply in love and knew that a life without experiencing this love would be a loss. This love ignited my desire for a family, a nest. I wanted kids and a place everyone could call home. As untraditional as I sometimes tend to be, and as this union was, I found myself wanting something very traditional. Family, home, and community. Starting out, I had a vision of what that might look like. My life collage is much different than that initial vision.

I do not believe that in having kids you are simply raising them to be independent adults. You are imprinting memories, impacting, for better or for worse, who they are and will be. Creating a history of their childhood and beyond. Within that history is the future answer to the common question on that first or second date: "What was your childhood like?"

A blended family is complicated and multilayered. It took me a while to discover and understand all the varied elements that make blended families distinctive. You are mixing together a group of individuals with different voices, diverse desires, and little, if any, backstory. It includes not only the folks now living under the same roof but also all the individuals who captivated their love and attention before you arrived on the scene.

A blended family is not two people walking away from a signed contract into the sunshine of one life. It is a multiple personality. It is unique. And it is within this uniqueness that the difficulty and the potential beauty lie.

Although no two blended families are alike, certain similarities exist. Holidays are hard. Common life milestones are complicated. The holidays and events that I used to look forward to have altered over the years. I still relish my mom's Christmas Eve celebrations with the Swedish smorgasbord and the tradition of reading notes to Santa before shooting them up our old family fireplace, but that tradition will be one for me, not for my blended-family memory bank.

Mother's Day is still a strange, retail-driven Sunday. Selfishly, I wish it did not exist. Forced acknowledgments are uncomfortable. Instead, I have created a space in my head to pardon myself on that weekend. Now, when I see May approaching, I honor my mother. I honor my stepkids' mother. And I honor myself. I forgive myself for my mistakes in mothering. I take time, as both a "wicked stepmother" and a mother, to be honorable and not awkward.

In hindsight, I wish that Art and I had thought about and created a special day for our immediate family. One that belonged only to us. No past history. No gifts. A family holiday, a date, to commemorate all of us every single year. An occasion that would create its own memories and allow a chance for future reminiscences built around this group of people. A slice of our own family history.


IN 1988, WHEN MY BROTHER Robert died, I became a member of a new club: the "siblings who have had a sibling die" club.

The same thing happened when I became a stepmother. And the stepmother club has a feel similar to that of the dead-sibling club. We stepmothers have a mutual understanding, without having to say a word. A wink and a nod, and we just know. The deepest and the darkest. The good and the bad.

The most common comment I have heard over the years when non-stepparents meet me for the first time is "How hard it must be to be a stepparent!" And it is. But the cliché is also true: even though they sometimes feel few and far between, hard things produce rewards. I have many. I have two people in my life who made me stronger. They challenged me. Rolled their eyes at me. Surprised me. I have more love in my life because of their presence. They have gifted me with smiles and hugs and small people who call me Granny. My life is better because of them.

I do not claim to be much of an expert at anything. In the past twenty-two years, almost half of my life, I have been a cook, large- and small-animal keeper, gardener, laundress, and supreme housecleaner. I have managed a medical practice, sold telecommunication services, and repped a clothing line.

But what I really have been, primarily, is a stepmom and a mom. This has been my career of sorts.

Early in this book, I mentioned that my personal shape is a circle. It is a circle of love without angles or corners. No chairs are removed. My brother's and my dad's chairs are still in place. My family sits there. This circle of love is my safe spot. You simply cannot have too much love in your life.

On the good days, I still believe this. But—if I am truly honest—there are days when I think all this love creates some conflicts. Stepkids are in a tough spot. When you first come into their lives, they may not really want you there. They liked things the old way. So all this love you are giving out may not really be something they want or know what to do with. And I honestly do not know if they can ever really trust it. What if I divorce their dad, too? Will I still love them? How could I possibly love them as much as I love my own child? Why do I love them? Is it a command performance because of the marriage certificate, or a real and true emotion?

Stepkids, I believe, also struggle internally with their

conflicted feelings about their real mother and their step-mother. I think it can take a long, long time to sort out these feelings, if they ever really do.

I am imperfect. Going into this, I had hopes and expecta-tions. And though my goal was, and is, always to give love or whatever else freely, I have over the years been disappointed, even crushed, if those hopes were misinterpreted, rejected, or ignored.

While I can hum the tune to that Helen Reddy song tell-ing me I am strong, wise, and unshakable, as a stepmom I have not always felt that way. Often I have felt uncertain and lonely. Sometimes I have felt like a bystander in my own home.

I said early on there was a time when I imagined it would simply work. But *simple* is not a word I would use in a sen-tence describing a stepmom and her role in a blended family.

Maybe we should do away with the whole term *step-mother*, which does not in any way explain the depth of the relationship, the complexities, the yin and the yang, the feel-ings, the sacrifices, or the compromises. It is not a word of comfort or of home. It does not provide a nest of warmth or protection. It has the possibility of setting up, from the mo-ment you apply the label, a competition. It is a clumsy word and an inadequate moniker.

It is a club I joined freely. But, as with a lot of clubs, I have had to step back in some areas of involvement. I no longer want to be on every subcommittee, if that makes sense. My relationship with my stepkids is complex and extraordi-nary. I love them both. They are both very different people with different ways of expressing themselves. My stepdaughter was in my face from day one with every emotion on the planet. My stepson was quieter, more calculated, with his emotions. Today, they still each have a chair in my circle. I still always think about their feelings and ambitions. I plan events with them in mind. I hope for quality conversations that rise above the mundane and elevate us into a relationship that is meaningful and heartfelt. And while I may not chair the next event, I will always be a member of the club. I've prepaid the dues.

In the first years of my marriage, I was told, *Wait it out. Everything will evolve. It will get better.* In the last few years, the biggest change for me has been that I no longer expect any change. I do not wait for more time to pass. I do not wait for anything. I find myself channeling the gal who met Art in the very beginning. Confident and unconcerned. Not always perfect, but someone who wakes up every day and tries to do the right thing for herself, her husband, and her family.

I used to sing a medley of songs to Marlowe before bed, rocking slowly back and forth, watching the lights across the valley from her bedroom window. The last song in my lineup was a song by Irving King that my dad used to sing to us, describing the drink he had a while ago and his desire to get on home. By the time I started singing it to Marlowe, I had forgotten most of the words and made up my own. It is a song for all the members of my family—Art, Ashton, Katherine, Marlowe, and me. No matter how far we go, how much we wander physically or emotionally, we will always know how to find our way home. The door will be open.

# ACKNOWLEDGMENTS

I would like to thank some people who do not even know they have helped me, starting with the kind counselor I saw briefly years ago, who, after our first visit, gave me an assignment to bring in a picture or object that explained how I felt at present. I went home and made a collage, and the door to that creative space in my brain that had been closed very tightly cracked open and the words tumbled out with a gasp.

Thanks to the many random and varied women I have overheard in grocery-store aisles or waiting in the post office line, speaking my language as they express their sadness, anger, or joy about their lives as stepmoms.

Thanks to Corbin Lewars, an early guide and editor, who, with a small group of women, did not shoot me down for my rambling narrative.

To Brooke Warner and all the folks at She Writes Press, and to Crystal Patriarche and her team at BookSparks, thanks for letting me be part of this club that you have created and built. I am grateful for your expertise and knowledge and for your introduction to the extremely talented authors who sit in the circle with me.

Huge gratitude to Annie Tucker, editor extraordinaire, randomly introduced to me from the universe of the Internet, only to turn out to be someone with whom I had much in common. You asked the right questions, prodded me with the right stick, and gently guided me away from the bad parts, all the while steadily bringing me to the last page. I could not have completed this without you.

To my brother and my sister: we have shared the same skies. Sibling love is the foundation of so much to follow. I am thankful ours is so strong.

Moms matter, and my mom matters to me. You have supported me from day one. You have been my prime example of what love and resiliency look like and what can happen if you simply show up. Thanks doesn't really say enough.

To my dad and my brother Robert, my two friendly ghosts who walk beside me, pat me on the back, and have taught me as much about life as they have about death.

To my three kids: you never asked me why I had to write this, and your faith in my decision means the world to me. The world would be smaller without you in my lives. I love you all.

There would not be a story without Art. You brought the kids. You (hardly ever) wavered in your support of this effort and rarely blinked at all the times I started and stopped and started again. Thanks for reading drafts when you did not want to, saying yes to most of my ideas, and believing in my abilities. Thanks for choosing me to complete our definition of family.

# ABOUT THE AUTHOR

photo credit: C. Sprenkle

Marianne Lile lives in Seattle, WA. She has been a step-mother and mother of three children for over twenty years. This is her first book.

Find her at www.mariannelile.com

# SELECTED TITLES FROM SHE WRITES PRESS

She Writes Press is an independent publishing company
founded to serve women writers everywhere.
Visit us at www.shewritespress.com.

*Make a Wish for Me: A Mother's Memoir* by LeeAndra Chergey. $16.95,
978-1-63152-828-6. A life-changing diagnosis teaches a family that
where's there is love there is hope—and that being "normal" is not
nearly as important as providing your child with a life full of joy,
love, and acceptance.

*A Leg to Stand On: An Amputee's Walk into Motherhood* by Colleen Hag-
gerty. $16.95, 978-1-63152-923-8. Haggerty's candid story of how
she overcame the pain of losing a leg at seventeen—and of terminat-
ing two pregnancies as a young woman—and went on to become a
mother, despite her fears.

*Splitting the Difference: A Heart-Shaped Memoir* by Tré Miller-Rodríguez.
$19.95, 978-1-938314-20-9. When 34-year-old Tré Miller-
Rodríguez's husband dies suddenly from a heart attack, her grief
sends her on an unexpected journey that culminates in a reunion
with the biological daughter she gave up at 18.

*The Doctor and The Stork: A Memoir of Modern Medical Babymaking* by
K.K. Goldberg. $16.95, 978-1-63152-830-9. A mother's compelling
story of her post-IVF, high-risk pregnancy with twins—the very
definition of a modern medical babymaking experience.

*Peanut Butter and Naan: Stories of an American Mother in The Far East*
by Jennifer Magnuson. $16.95, 978-1-63152-911-5. The hilarious
tale of what happened when Jennifer Magnuson moved her family of
seven from Nashville to India in an effort to shake things up—and
got more than she bargained for.

*Science of Parenthood: Thoroughly Unscientific Explanations for Utterly
Baffling Parenting Situations* by Norine Dworkin-McDaniel and Jes-
sica Ziegler. $19.95, 978-1-63152-947-4. A satirical take on the early
years of parenting that uses faux math, snarky science, and irreverent
cartoons to offer hilarious hypotheses for parenting's most perplex-
ing mysteries.